# THE MANY DEATHS OF THE BATMAN™

# THE MANY DEATHS OF THE BATMAN™

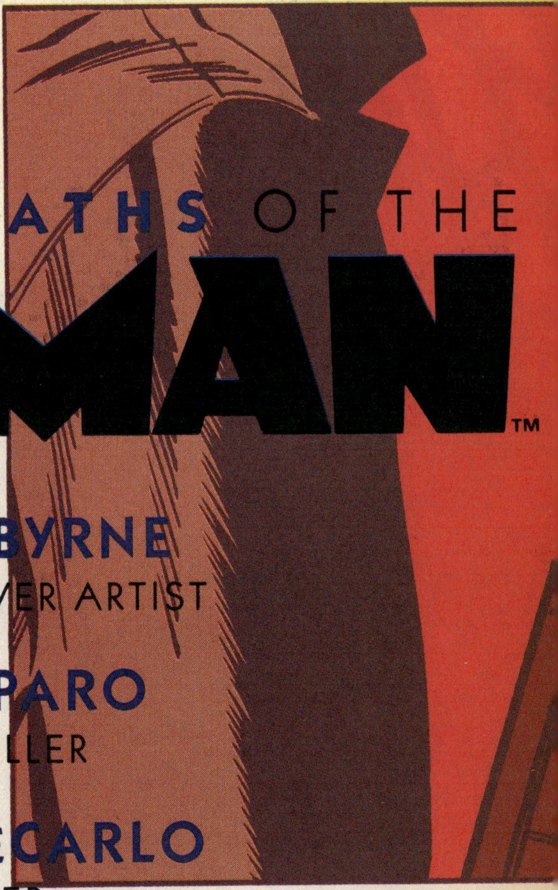

**JOHN BYRNE**
WRITER/COVER ARTIST

**JIM APARO**
PENCILLER

**MIKE DeCARLO**
INKER

**JOHN COSTANZA**
LETTERER

**ADRIENNE ROY**
COLORIST

BATMAN CREATED BY **BOB KANE**

PULL HANDLE DOWN
GOTH
NEWS
BATMAN DEAD

**BATMAN: THE MANY DEATHS OF THE BATMAN**


DC Comics Inc., 1325 Avenue of the Americas, New York, NY 10019
A Warner Bros. Inc. Company
Printed in Canada. First Printing.
ISBN: 1-56389-033-X

Front cover illustration by John Byrne
Back cover illustration by Jim Aparo
Publication design by Brian Pearce

# INTRODUCTION

I'm a little bit strange.

I've never seen Hitchcock's *The Lady Vanishes,* but I can tell you countless stories about its filming. I've never read Dante's *Divine Comedy,* but I could go on for hours about its marriage of medieval literature's saintly and courtly love traditions. To this day I've never heard Gershwin's *Rhapsody in Blue,* but I could write an essay on how it made use of rag and other jazz piano styles.

You see, I suffer from an unusual disease: I'm one of those people who enjoy learning *about* something more than they enjoy the thing itself. More specifically, I find the *creation* of a work of art more interesting than the finished product. If you learn enough about the genesis of a work, you can get into the artist's head and vicariously experience the same thrill of discovery that they did at the moment of the worker's creation.

Fortunately for me, I'm not alone. In fact, there're quite a few of us who feel this way. Those *The Making of [movie x]* specials on cable? They're marketed for us. Those "story behind the story" books? Us again. Hell, the entire field of literary criticism might have died out with some obscure Talmudic scholar if not for people like me.

So when collected editions editor Michael Hill asked me to write the introduction to "The Many Deaths of the Batman," I jumped at the chance. Here was an opportunity to write something designed for me and others like me.

You see, for people like me, the ultimate authority on any work of art is the artist himself. Why bother listening to anyone else? Let's say there's a *Citizen Kane* symposium. On your left are Siskel & Ebert giving their critiques. On your right is the disembodied voice of Orson Welles critiquing from beyond the grave. You'd turn to your right, right? Why mess around when you can go straight to the source?

So straight to the source is where I went, and that's where my year of experience as the assistant editor on BATMAN and DETECTIVE COMICS paid off, because the one important thing I learned at DC is...

...phone numbers. Denny O'Neil's, John Byrne's, and Jim Aparo's, to be exact. After a little schedule-juggling and telephone tag, these three gracious gentlemen granted me the interviews that follow.

So for those of you who share my affliction, read on and feast yourselves on the abundant creative insights contained within.

And for those of you of a more traditional bent, skip the next two pages and dig in—it's a hell of a story.

**BY KELLEY PUCKETT**

I notice that "The Many Deaths of the Batman" was published in early 1989, at about the same time as Sam Hamm and Denys Cowan's "Blind Justice" miniseries, which also dealt with characters from Batman's shadowy past. Was there some sort of editorial directive to John Byrne to write such a story?

# DENNY O'NEIL

**"No. The story was John's idea. But at that time we were engaged in filling in the backstory of Batman's origin. So, one of the reasons I approved the project was that that was what we were doing that year."**

What was your reaction when John said he wanted to do a silent first issue?

**"My reaction was positive. I had a lot of faith that Jim could pull it off. In fact, I think I had more faith in Jim than Jim did.**

**"I think we should push the envelope every once in a while. I'd done a silent issue once before for another company, and I was pleased with the outcome."**

# JOHN BYRNE

How did this whole project come about?

**"Denny asked me if I had three issues' worth of story 'cause there were three issues of BATMAN to fill.**

**"I had had an idea in the back of my head to do an old-fashioned Batman story but with a modern twist. I remembered a classic story where there were these con artists convincing rich people that there were many Batmans, trying to sell them costumes—you, too, can be a Batman!**

**"Of course, if we do it modern, they'd all be killing people. So I got the idea of using the people who *trained* Batman and having somebody knocking them off."**

Why the silent issue?

**"I like to do silent issues. Comics are a visual medium and I like to exploit that. Silent issues are the best way to do that, to exploit the visual medium.**

**"I didn't know when I was writing it that Jim Aparo would be the artist, or I would've done it completely silent. Not knowing who was going to draw it, I didn't have faith that the artist could pull off a "Get out," so I put that one bit of dialogue in. If I had known it was gong to be Jim Aparo, I would've left it out."**

Had your own experience as an artist helped you with the special requirements of writing a silent issue?

**"Way back when—about a hundred years ago—I did one for "The Art of John Byrne." That was my first silent story. I intended it for a twelve-page story, but it ended up being**

twenty-five pages.

**"I soon realized that I couldn't just say "Later...." I had to somehow *show* it getting later. I learned from that. I knew I had to provide visual bridges to Jim Aparo for the story."**

# JIM APARO

How did you react when you found out part one was a silent issue?

**"I really like doing silent issues. It puts you in a position to do more things. You're like a movie director. You've got to show all the stuff.**

**"Say you want to show a man walking into a room. Normally, you would say, 'He walked in,' and just show the guy in the room with the door open. But when you do it with no dialogue, you gotta show the hand turning the knob, the door opening, all that stuff. It's like a silent movie.**

**"It's more of a challenge for the artist. You have to draw a lot of stuff that the dialogue usually covers. A silent story gives the artist more...he has to draw more to get the point across. It really shows the power of illustration."**

Was this your first silent issue?

**"There was a story—I believe it was in HOUSE OF MYSTERY—a science-fiction story called "The Singling." I think the writer was Gerald Brown. I'm not sure. That was a six-pager, science fiction with aliens, and that had no talking. That story was written out, broken down by panels. He told me what to draw."**

What was the format of John's script?

**"John Byrne wrote his story in paragraphs, like a book. It was about three pages and I read it and started breaking it down, panel by panel."**

My favorite part of the issue is the hospital scene. What was in the script for that scene?

**"All Byrne gave me was that they wheeled him in. You know, everybody looks shocked. He mentioned the monitor to me. I added some extra panels. I had to work to keep all that material in one page. He as the writer would mention these things, but I had to carry it over, space out the panels to keep up suspense. You know, you just give the artist the idea and he conveys the emotions: remorse, sadness, shock."**

***Kelley Puckett** is a writer, and former assistant editor of BATMAN and DETECTIVE COMICS.*

THE MANY DEATHS OF THE BATMAN
CHAPTER ONE: PERIOD OF MOURNING
WHEEEEEEEEEEEEE

POLICE

THIS END UP
3

WHREEEEEEEEEEEEEE
AMBULANCE
GOTHAM GENERAL HOSPITAL
EMERG

EMERGE
AMBULANCE
ENTRANCE

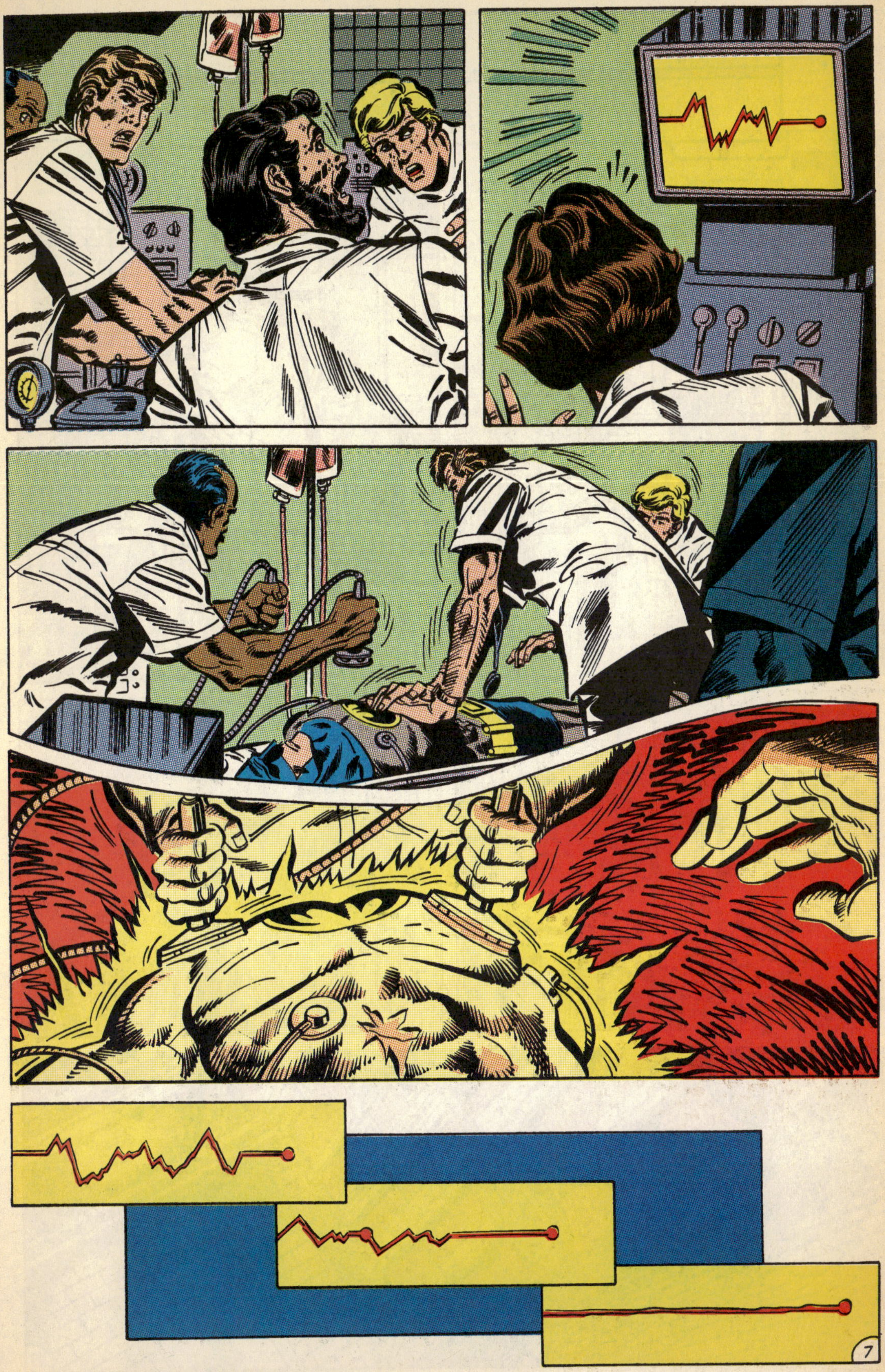

MORGUE

CAFETERIA

MORGUE

EXTRA
GOTHAM NEWS
EXTRA
BATMAN DEAD
STORY AND PHOTOS ON PAGE THREE

ARKHAM
ASYLUM
SALE
DEAD
13

NEWS
EXTRA

PULL HANDLE DOWN
BATMAN DEAD

16

EXTRA
BATMAN
DEAD
GOTHAM NEWS

AIRMOU
WELCOME NATION
CONVENTION OF POLICE
COMMISSIONERS

POLICE
GOTHAM
GENERAL
HOSPITAL
EMERGENC
GET OUT.

GOTHAM
PLAZA
HOTEL

2

4

Chapter Two: HOW MANY TIMES CAN A BATMAN DIE?
GOTHAM CITY, USA. 5:30 AM
POLI

DEAD.
BEEN DEAD ABOUT EIGHT HOURS, I'D GUESS. RIGOR STILL IN EVIDENCE...
DROWNED? OR IS THAT TOO OBVIOUS?
HARD TO SAY FOR SURE, WITHOUT AN AUTOPSY.
FUNNY... SOMEHOW THAT'S NOT AT ALL THE WAY I WOULD HAVE EXPECTED THEM TO GO.
IT ISN'T.
HOLD ON A MINUTE, YOU MEN.
I KNOW THAT FACE...
THAT'S MARK JENNER!
YES, I THOUGHT HE LOOKED FAMILIAR.
ONCE UPON A TIME AMERICA'S GREATEST STOCK CAR RACER. WON ALL THE CUPS THERE WERE TO WIN EIGHT OR NINE YEARS AGO.
BUT... HOW THE HELL CAN MARK JENNER BE THE BATMAN?
HE WAS PARALYZED IN A CAR CRASH FIVE YEARS AGO!
YES.
BUT I DON'T THINK THIS IS REALLY BATMAN.
WHY NOT? NOW THAT I THINK ABOUT IT, FAKE PARALYSIS WOULD BE A PERFECT COVER...
I SUPPOSE IT WOULD.
THERE'S JUST ONE SMALL SNAG IN YOUR THEORY, DOCTOR...
THIS IS THE FOURTH DEAD "BATMAN" WE'VE TURNED UP IN THE LAST TWELVE HOURS...

THE OFFICE OF THE POLICE COMMISSIONER, SIX HOURS LATER.
IT JUST DOESN'T MAKE SENSE.
NONE OF IT MAKES SENSE.
FOUR DEAD MEN. EACH ONE AN EXPERT IN HIS PARTICULAR FIELD.
JENNER, THE EXPERT DRIVER. STONE, THE DEMOLITION EXPERT. KINGSLEY, THE CHEMISTRY WHIZ. LA SALLE, THE BODY BUILDER.
SEVEN OR EIGHT YEARS AGO THIS WOULD HAVE BEEN A VIRTUAL WHO'S WHO OF THE WORLD'S WUNDERKIND.
WHY WOULD ANYONE WANT TO KILL THEM?
AND, MAYBE MORE SIGNIFICANTLY, WHY WOULD ANYONE WANT TO DRESS THEM UP AS THE BATMAN BEFORE...
NOK NOK
COME...
HOPE I'M NOT DISTURBING YOU, COMMISSIONER. I THOUGHT YOU'D WANT TO SEE THIS REPORT ON JENNER A.S.A.P.
I DO...
BUT A PHONE CALL OR A MESSENGER WOULD HAVE SUFFICED FOR NOW, DOCTOR. NO NEED FOR YOU TO COME YOURSELF.
I SUPPOSE NOT, BUT THIS BUSINESS INTRIGUES ME.
MAYBE I'VE BEEN WATCHING TOO MANY RE-RUNS OF "QUINCY," BUT I THOUGHT I'D LIKE TO GET A LITTLE MORE... HANDS ON EXPERIENCE ON THIS CASE.
I WOULDN'T HAVE THOUGHT IT WOULD BE POSSIBLE TO GET MORE "HANDS-ON" THAN YOUR LINE OF WORK, DOCTOR.
TRUE...
BUT THERE'S A SAYING IN MY PROFESSION THAT THE PATHOLOGIST "KNOWS EVERYTHING, BUT ALWAYS TOO LATE." I THOUGHT I'D LIKE TO BE IN ON THIS A LITTLE, WELL, SOONER THAN I USUALLY AM.
BEFORE SOMEONE DIES, FOR INSTANCE.
IF YOU CAN FIGURE OUT A WAY TO DO THAT, DOCTOR, PLEASE LET ME KNOW. IT WOULD MAKE MY JOB A LOT EASIER.
AS WOULD READING THESE REPORTS IF THEY WERE IN ENGLISH. WHAT'S ALL THIS ABOUT THE CONTENT OF THE LUNGS...?
IT WAS FRESH WATER. TAP WATER, I'D SAY.
WHEREVER MR. JENNER DROWNED, IT WASN'T IN THE RIVER.
7

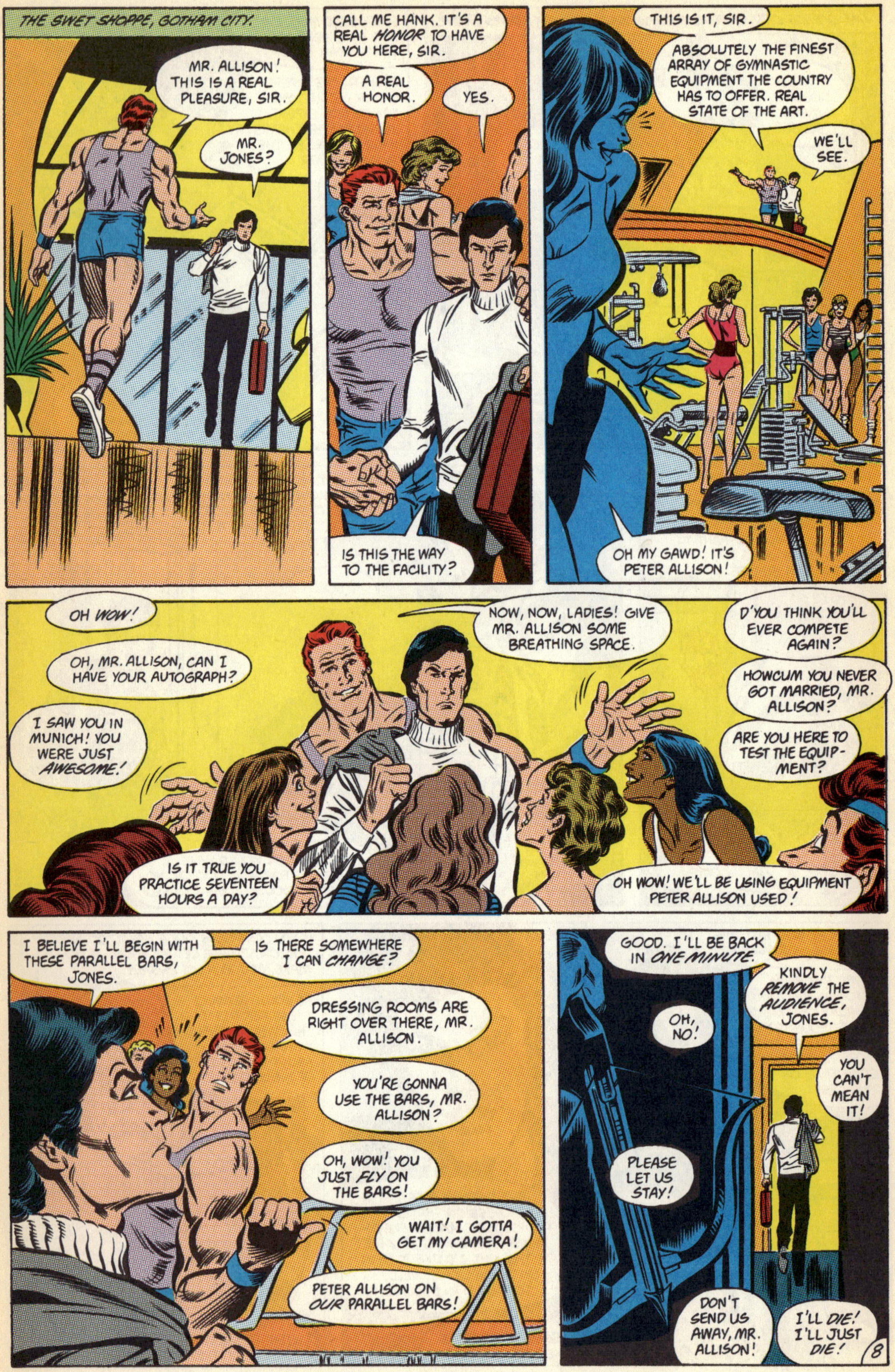
THE SWEET SHOPPE, GOTHAM CITY.
MR. ALLISON! THIS IS A REAL PLEASURE, SIR.
MR. JONES?
CALL ME HANK. IT'S A REAL *HONOR* TO HAVE YOU HERE, SIR.
A REAL HONOR.
YES.
IS THIS THE WAY TO THE FACILITY?
THIS IS IT, SIR.
ABSOLUTELY THE FINEST ARRAY OF GYMNASTIC EQUIPMENT THE COUNTRY HAS TO OFFER. REAL STATE OF THE ART.
WE'LL SEE.
OH MY GAWD! IT'S PETER ALLISON!
OH *WOW!*
OH, MR. ALLISON, CAN I HAVE YOUR AUTOGRAPH?
I SAW YOU IN MUNICH! YOU WERE JUST *AWESOME!*
NOW, NOW, LADIES! GIVE MR. ALLISON SOME BREATHING SPACE.
D'YOU THINK YOU'LL EVER COMPETE AGAIN?
HOWCUM YOU NEVER GOT MARRIED, MR. ALLISON?
ARE YOU HERE TO TEST THE EQUIPMENT?
IS IT TRUE YOU PRACTICE SEVENTEEN HOURS A DAY?
OH WOW! WE'LL BE USING EQUIPMENT PETER ALLISON USED!
I BELIEVE I'LL BEGIN WITH THESE PARALLEL BARS, JONES.
IS THERE SOMEWHERE I CAN *CHANGE?*
DRESSING ROOMS ARE RIGHT OVER THERE, MR. ALLISON.
YOU'RE GONNA USE THE BARS, MR. ALLISON?
OH, WOW! YOU JUST *FLY* ON THE BARS!
WAIT! I GOTTA GET MY CAMERA!
PETER ALLISON ON *OUR* PARALLEL BARS!
GOOD. I'LL BE BACK IN *ONE MINUTE.*
KINDLY *REMOVE* THE *AUDIENCE,* JONES.
OH, NO!
YOU CAN'T MEAN IT!
PLEASE LET US STAY!
DON'T SEND US AWAY, MR. ALLISON!
I'LL *DIE!* I'LL JUST *DIE!*

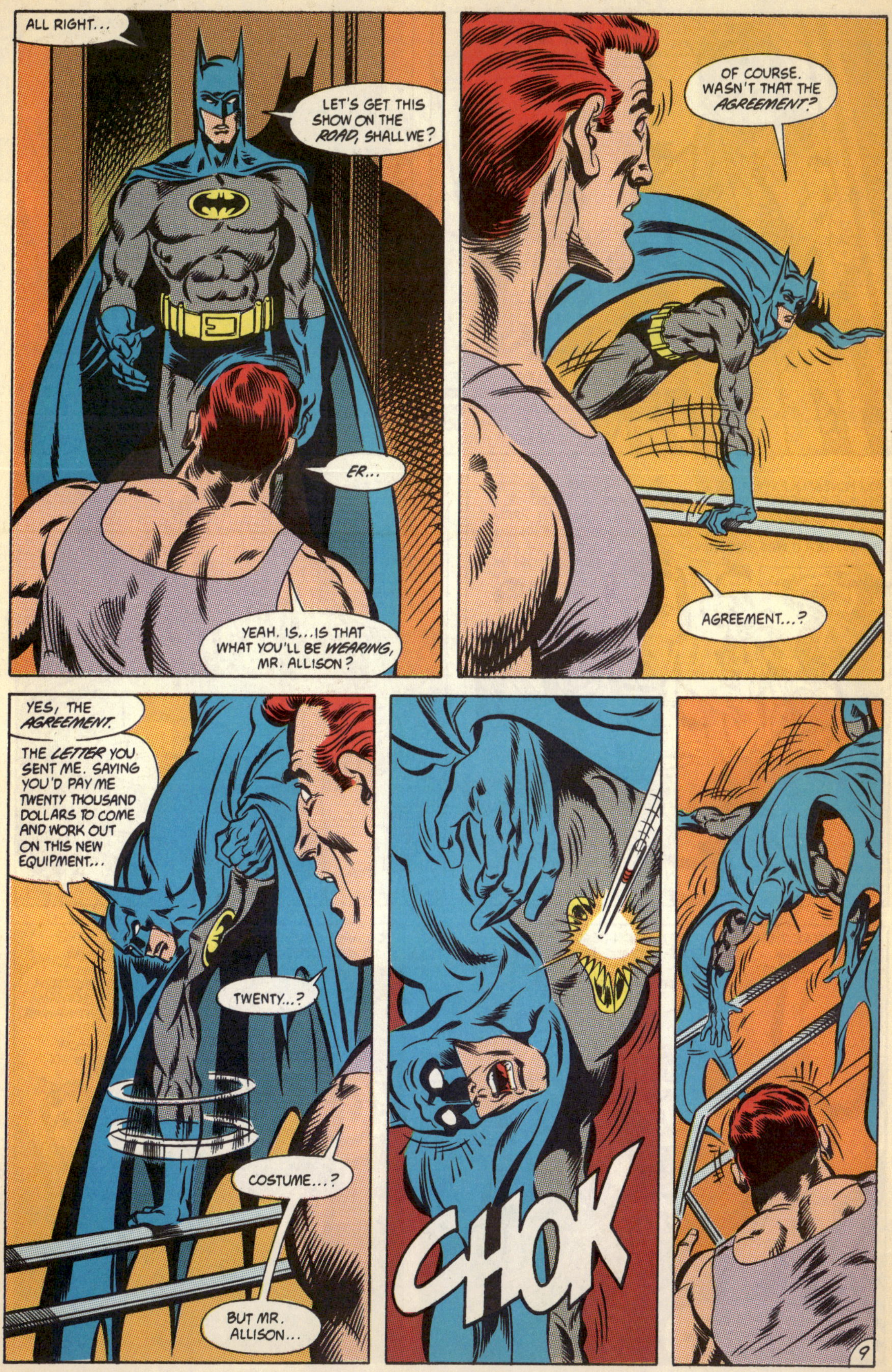
ALL RIGHT...
LET'S GET THIS SHOW ON THE *ROAD*, SHALL WE?
ER...
YEAH. IS...IS THAT WHAT YOU'LL BE *WEARING*, MR. ALLISON?
OF COURSE. WASN'T THAT THE *AGREEMENT*?
AGREEMENT...?
YES, THE *AGREEMENT*.
THE *LETTER* YOU SENT ME. SAYING YOU'D PAY ME TWENTY THOUSAND DOLLARS TO COME AND WORK OUT ON THIS NEW EQUIPMENT...
TWENTY...?
COSTUME...?
BUT MR. ALLISON...
CHOK
9

WHOEVER DID THIS REALLY WANTED HIM DEAD.
THIS ARROW HAS BEEN POISONED.
A CLASSIC CASE OF OVERKILL, DOCTOR. I'M SURE THAT CROSS-BOW BOLT DID THE JOB PERFECTLY WELL.
AND NOW YOU'VE GOT ANOTHER DEAD BATMAN ON YOUR HANDS.
YES. NUMBER FIVE.
JONES... YOU'RE SURE YOU SAW NO ONE?
NOT A LIVING SOUL, SIR.
YOU HONESTLY EXPECT ME TO BELIEVE SOMEONE WALKED IN HERE WITH A CROSSBOW, SHOT THIS MAN, AND WALKED OUT AGAIN? AND YOU HAD NO IDEA IT WAS HAPPENING?
N-NOSSIR. IF ANYONE CAME IN IT MUST'VE BEEN BEFORE I ARRIVED. I JUST DON'T KNOW HOW HE GOT OUT OF THAT SUPPLY CLOSET...
I THINK I'VE GOT THE ANSWER ON THAT ONE, COMMISSIONER.
THAT VENT WAS COVERED UP WITH THESE EQUIPMENT BOXES.
WHOEVER DID THIS MUST'VE DONE HIS HOMEWORK.
I'LL SAY! I NEVER KNEW THAT VENT WAS THERE!
HE DID MORE THAN HIS HOMEWORK.
TO HIT ALLISON DEAD CENTER IN THE HEART--MOVING TARGET, ACROSS THE GYM--I SUSPECT YOU'D HAVE TO BE PRETTY HANDY WITH A WEAPON LIKE THIS TO DO THAT.
HEY, THAT'S RIGHT! WHY DIDN'T I THINK OF THAT BEFORE!
YOU HAVE SOMETHING TO ADD, JONES?
SURE! IT WAS ON THE TV THIS MORNING.
RAPHAEL DIGIORDA ARRIVED IN GOTHAM LAST NIGHT. HE WAS OLYMPIC CROSSBOW CHAMPION SIX, SEVEN YEARS AGO..
10

POLICE

BATMAN, MORT!

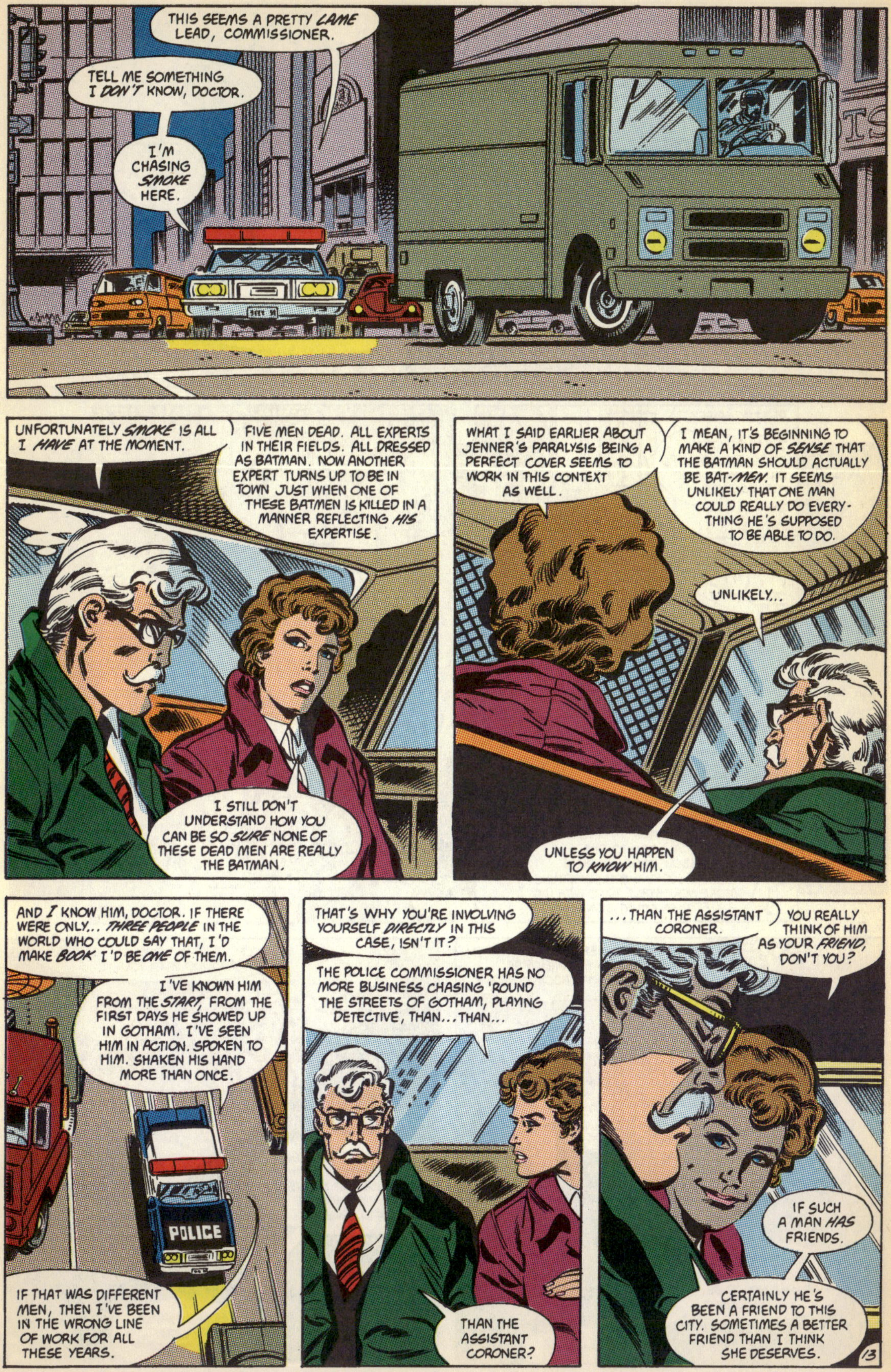
THIS SEEMS A PRETTY LAME LEAD, COMMISSIONER.
TELL ME SOMETHING I DON'T KNOW, DOCTOR.
I'M CHASING SMOKE HERE.
UNFORTUNATELY SMOKE IS ALL I HAVE AT THE MOMENT.
FIVE MEN DEAD. ALL EXPERTS IN THEIR FIELDS. ALL DRESSED AS BATMAN. NOW ANOTHER EXPERT TURNS UP TO BE IN TOWN JUST WHEN ONE OF THESE BATMEN IS KILLED IN A MANNER REFLECTING HIS EXPERTISE.
I STILL DON'T UNDERSTAND HOW YOU CAN BE SO SURE NONE OF THESE DEAD MEN ARE REALLY THE BATMAN.
WHAT I SAID EARLIER ABOUT JENNER'S PARALYSIS BEING A PERFECT COVER SEEMS TO WORK IN THIS CONTEXT AS WELL.
I MEAN, IT'S BEGINNING TO MAKE A KIND OF SENSE THAT THE BATMAN SHOULD ACTUALLY BE BAT-MEN. IT SEEMS UNLIKELY THAT ONE MAN COULD REALLY DO EVERYTHING HE'S SUPPOSED TO BE ABLE TO DO.
UNLIKELY...
UNLESS YOU HAPPEN TO KNOW HIM.
AND I KNOW HIM, DOCTOR. IF THERE WERE ONLY... THREE PEOPLE IN THE WORLD WHO COULD SAY THAT, I'D MAKE BOOK I'D BE ONE OF THEM.
I'VE KNOWN HIM FROM THE START, FROM THE FIRST DAYS HE SHOWED UP IN GOTHAM. I'VE SEEN HIM IN ACTION. SPOKEN TO HIM. SHAKEN HIS HAND MORE THAN ONCE.
POLICE
IF THAT WAS DIFFERENT MEN, THEN I'VE BEEN IN THE WRONG LINE OF WORK FOR ALL THESE YEARS.
THAT'S WHY YOU'RE INVOLVING YOURSELF DIRECTLY IN THIS CASE, ISN'T IT?
THE POLICE COMMISSIONER HAS NO MORE BUSINESS CHASING 'ROUND THE STREETS OF GOTHAM, PLAYING DETECTIVE, THAN... THAN...
THAN THE ASSISTANT CORONER?
... THAN THE ASSISTANT CORONER.
YOU REALLY THINK OF HIM AS YOUR FRIEND, DON'T YOU?
IF SUCH A MAN HAS FRIENDS.
CERTAINLY HE'S BEEN A FRIEND TO THIS CITY. SOMETIMES A BETTER FRIEND THAN I THINK SHE DESERVES.

WHAT WAS ALL THAT ABOUT ALLISON GETTING SOME KIND OF LETTER FROM JONES?
AND JONES A LETTER FROM ALLISON.
IT SEEMS OUR LATE MR. ALLISON WAS EXPECTING TO GET *PAID* RATHER A LOT OF MONEY FOR HIS APPEARANCE AT THE "*SWET SHOPPE*," WHILE MR. JONES BELIEVED ALLISON WAS *VOLUNTEERING* HIS NAME AND REPUTATION.
CLEVER. PLAYED OFF JONES'S GULLIBILITY AND ALLISON'S ARROGANCE *PERFECTLY*.
WE'RE *HERE*, COMMISSIONER.
PRETTY SPIFFY.
I HAD NO IDEA CROSSBOW CHAMPS DID SO *WELL* FOR THEMSELVES.
THEY DO IF THEY'RE RAPHAEL DIGIORDA. HIS FAMILY IS ONE OF THE *RICHEST* IN ITALY. DIGIORDA GOT INTO THIS CROSSBOW THING BECAUSE HE WAS LOOKING FOR SOMETHING MORE WORTHWHILE TO DO WITH HIS LIFE THAN COUNT MONEY.
LET'S FIND OUT WHAT'S HAPPENING WITH MR. DIGIORDA...
ASSUMING HE HASN'T *SKIPPED TOWN* AFTER COMMITTING THE LAST MURDER?
I'M COMMISSIONER JAMES GORDON. IT'S *VITAL* I SEE MR. DIGIORDA IMMEDIATELY. WHAT ROOM IS HE IN?
MR. DIGIORDA LEFT *STRICT* INSTRUCTIONS HE WAS NOT TO BE DISTURBED.
BY *ANYONE*.
LOOK, I'M IN NO MOOD TO MESS AROUND WITH YOU.
DIGIORDA IS WANTED FOR QUESTIONING IN A *MURDER*. AT THE VERY LEAST HIS OWN LIFE MAY BE IN DANGER.
*NOW WHAT'S HIS ROOM NUMBER??*

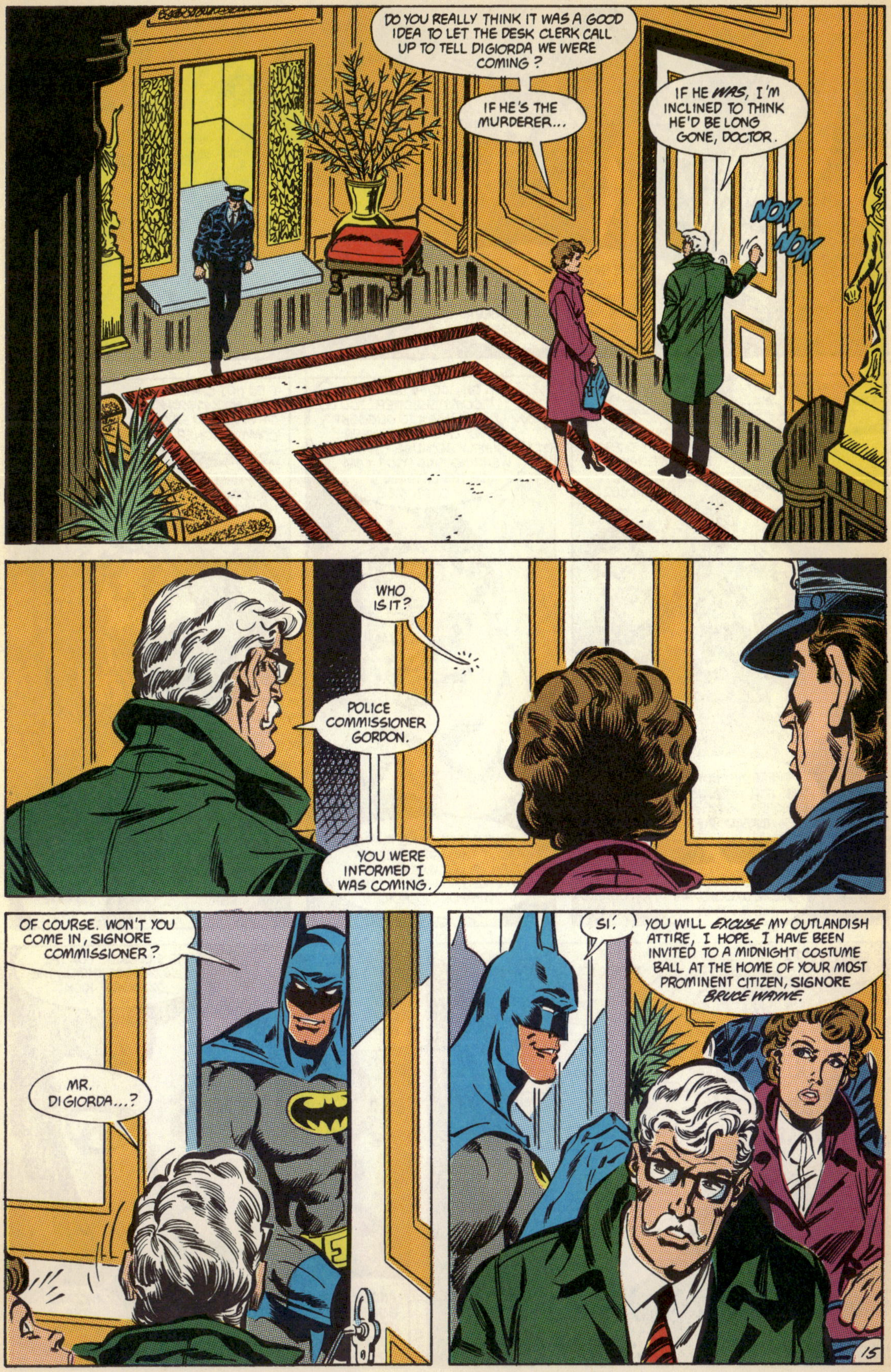
DO YOU REALLY THINK IT WAS A GOOD IDEA TO LET THE DESK CLERK CALL UP TO TELL DIGIORDA WE WERE COMING?
IF HE'S THE MURDERER...
IF HE *WAS*, I'M INCLINED TO THINK HE'D BE LONG GONE, DOCTOR.
NOK NOK
WHO IS IT?
POLICE COMMISSIONER GORDON.
YOU WERE INFORMED I WAS COMING.
OF COURSE. WON'T YOU COME IN, SIGNORE COMMISSIONER?
MR. DIGIORDA...?
SI!
YOU WILL *EXCUSE* MY OUTLANDISH ATTIRE, I HOPE. I HAVE BEEN INVITED TO A MIDNIGHT COSTUME BALL AT THE HOME OF YOUR MOST PROMINENT CITIZEN, SIGNORE *BRUCE WAYNE*.
15

YOU KNOW MR. WAYNE?
TO THE BEST OF MY KNOWLEDGE, WE HAVE NEVER MET. HOWEVER, HE SENT A VERY FLATTERING NOTE, EXPRESSING A DESIRE TO MEET ME, ALONG WITH THIS COSTUME.
MR. WAYNE SENT YOU THAT COSTUME, MR. DIGIORDA?
SI!..
PARDON, LOVELY LADY, BUT I DO NOT THINK WE HAVE BEEN PROPERLY INTRODUCED...
THERE MAY NOT BE ANY TIME FOR INTRODUCTIONS, MR. DIGIORDA. FIVE MEN HAVE ALREADY DIED...
AND ALL OF THEM WERE DRESSED AS THE BATMAN.
HA HA HA!
OH, COME NOW, COMMISSIONER! YOU DO NOT MEAN TO SUGGEST MY LIFE IS IN DANGER? SIMPLY BECAUSE I AM WEARING THIS POOR COPY OF THE BATMAN'S COSTUME?
THERE'S NOTHING FUNNY ABOUT THIS, SIR. THE LAST MAN KILLED WAS SHOT WITH A CROSSBOW BOLT--YOUR WEAPON OF CHOICE.
I DO NOT CARE FOR THE IMPLICATION OF WHAT YOU SAY, COMMISSIONER.
RAPHAEL DIGIORDA IS NO MURDERER.
I'M NOT SAYING YOU ARE, MR. DIGIORDA...
BUT MAYBE BRUCE WAYNE IS!!
WHAT??
WHAT IN THE WORLD DO YOU THINK YOU'RE SAYING, DOCTOR?
DON'T YOU SEE, COMMISSIONER? IT MAKES SENSE...
THE MILLIONAIRE PLAYBOY... BORED... LOOKING FOR SOME NEW GAME TO SPARK SOME INTEREST IN HIS JADED LIFE...
MAYBE HE'S TRIED EVERYTHING ELSE. BIG GAME HUNTING. SKY DIVING. FAST CARS. FAST WOMEN. DRUGS.
HE'S LOOKING FOR THE ULTIMATE THRILL, THE ULTIMATE KICK.
AND HERE IN GOTHAM CITY THAT COULD REALLY ONLY BE ONE THING: BESTING THE BATMAN.
KILLING THE BATMAN!
16

AND YOU EXPECT ME TO BELIEVE THIS MAN... THE MAN WHO TURNED THE WAYNE FOUNDATION INTO ONE OF THE FINEST CHARITABLE INSTITUTIONS IN THIS COUNTRY...
THE MAN WHOM ANYONE WILL TELL YOU IS ONE OF THE FINEST CITIZENS IN GOTHAM...
... THIS MAN WOULD HAVE TURNED INTO A COLD BLOODED KILLER, JUST BECAUSE HE'S BORED?
WHY NOT?
IT WOULDN'T BE THE FIRST TIME A RESPECTED PUBLIC FIGURE HAS TURNED OUT TO HAVE FEET OF CLAY.
A COUPLE OF PRESIDENTS SPRING TO MIND. AND WHAT ABOUT LEX LUTHOR, IN METROPOLIS? HE'S SUPPOSED TO BE A LIVING SAINT, BUT I'VE HEARD HE'S NOT SO SQUEAKY CLEAN AS HE'D LIKE PEOPLE TO THINK.
THAT'S AS MAY BE...
AND AS FAR AS I'M CONCERNED IT HAS NOTHING TO DO WITH...
UH-HHHN..
MR. DIGIORDA...?
DIGIORDA!!
CRASH
HE'S... DEAD!
17

GOTHAM CITY POLICE MORGUE, SEVEN HOURS LATER--
WELL...?
POISONED.
SOMETHING IN THE COSTUME. A CURARE DERIVATIVE, I'D GUESS.
IT WAS ACTIVATED BY HIS OWN PERSPIRATION. PENETRATED THROUGH HIS PORES.
HE WAS DYING THE WHOLE TIME WE WERE THERE.
DYING WHILE WE WERE STANDING AROUND ARGUING...
YOU WANTED TO SEE POLICE WORK UP CLOSE. ONE OF THE FIRST THINGS YOU NEED TO LEARN IS THAT NONE OF US ARE PSYCHIC.
THERE'D BE A LOT LESS CRIME IF WE WERE. BUT WE'RE NOT.
THERE WAS NOTHING YOU COULD HAVE DONE.
I KNOW. IT'S JUST...
WHAT DO YOU PLAN TO DO NOW, COMMISSIONER?
NOW I PLAN TO PAY A VISIT TO BRUCE WAYNE.
WAYNE...?
BUT I THOUGHT...
I MEAN, YOU SAID...
I KNOW WHAT I SAID. AND I HAVEN'T CHANGED MY MIND. I STILL THINK BRUCE WAYNE IS COMPLETELY INNOCENT OF ANY CONNECTION TO THESE KILLINGS.
BUT THE DEATH OF PETER ALLISON LED US DIRECTLY TO RAPHAEL DIGIORDA...
"...AND DIGIORDA'S DEATH SEEMS TO BE LEADING US STRAIGHT TO BRUCE WAYNE."
WAYNE MANOR
POLICE
GOTHAM POLICE
COMMISSIONER GORDON TO SEE MR. WAYNE...
ER...YES, CERTAINLY. COME RIGHT UP.
18

GOOD MORNING, ALFRED. SORRY TO DROP IN ON YOU UNEXPECTEDLY LIKE THIS, BUT I NEED TO TALK TO MR. WAYNE ON A MATTER OF UTMOST URGENCY.
ER, YES, COMMISSIONER...
IT'S JUST THAT I'M NOT SURE THAT'S ENTIRELY POSSIBLE JUST AT THE MOMENT.
NOT POSSIBLE?
WHY NOT? HE'S HERE, ISN'T HE?
YES, SIR...
THAT IS, I BELIEVE SO. IT'S JUST THAT MR. WAYNE GOT IN VERY LATE LAST NIGHT, AND I DON'T KNOW...
THAT'S QUITE ALL RIGHT, ALFRED.
I'M ALWAYS PREPARED TO SEE THE COMMISSIONER.
WHAT CAN I DO FOR YOU? FROM THE LOOKS ON THE FACES OF YOUR COMPANIONS I GET THE FEELING THIS IS NOT A SOCIAL VISIT.
NO, IT ISN'T, WAYNE.
SOON--
SIX MEN MURDERED... ALL IN BATMAN COSTUMES...
AND MYSELF IMPLICATED IN THE MOST RECENT KILLINGS? OUTRAGEOUS!
I DIDN'T SAY YOU WERE IMPLICATED.
BUT THERE IS REASON TO THINK YOU MAY BE NEXT.
I CAN'T IMAGINE WHY. SURELY THERE'S NOTHING TO CONNECT ANY OF THESE MEN TO MYSELF, TO THE BATMAN...
ALFRED... NO ONE HAS SENT ME A BATMAN COSTUME LATELY, HAVE THEY...
WELL... NOT THAT I KNOW OF, SIR.
ALTHOUGH THERE IS THE PACKAGE THAT CAME WITH THE MORNING'S MAIL. IT'S BIG ENOUGH FOR SUCH A THING, I SUPPOSE...
19

I'D JUST BROUGHT THE MAIL IN WHEN THE COMMISSIONER ARRIVED.
THE PACKAGE IS RIGHT...
DON'T TOUCH THAT!
IF IT IS FROM THE KILLER, IT COULD BE BOOBY-TRAPPED!
ACME COSTUMIERS
AND YET, IF THIS MADMAN MEANS TO KILL ME IN THE SAME WAY AS THE OTHERS I NEED TO BE ABLE TO OPEN THE PACKAGE...
...AND PUT ON THE COSTUME, IF THERE'S REALLY ONE IN THERE.
IT LOOKS HARMLESS ENOUGH.
ORDINARY PAPER. ORDINARY PACKING TAPE.
MAYBE WE SHOULD SEND FOR THE BOMB SQUAD...?
THERE'S NO TRIGGERING MECHANISM IN THE WRAPPINGS...
AT LEAST NOTHING I CAN SEE.
AND AS I SAID...
...IF OUR ALLEGED KILLER IS HOLDING TRUE TO FORM...
...AND IT APPEARS HE IS...
...NOTHING IS GOING TO HAPPEN UNTIL I PUT THIS THING ON.
I CAN'T POSSIBLY ALLOW YOU TO DO THAT...
20

I DON'T INTEND TO COMMISSIONER.
I MAY BE IDLE, BUT I'M NOT ADDLED...
CLATTER
WELL... AT LEAST THAT WASN'T EXPLOSIVE.
IF IT HAD BEEN, WE'D ALL BE ADDING TO THE DECORATIONS ON YOUR VERY EXPENSIVE WALLS, MR. WAYNE.
PERHAPS.
STILL, WE SEEM TO HAVE CONFIRMATION OF YOUR THEORY, COMMISSIONER. I AM NEXT ON...
HMMM...
WHAT IS IT, CHAMBERS?
FUNNY SORT OF LOCK ON THIS BUCKLE.
I CAN'T SEEM TO... OH, THERE IT IS...
NO, DON'T...!
GIVE ME THAT!!
THIS BUSINESS HAS GOT US ALL SPOOKED!
NOT WITHOUT GOOD REASON, I'D SAY, COMMISSIONER.
IF THERE WAS AN EXPLOSIVE OR SOME OTHER SUCH LETHAL DEVICE IN THAT BELT...
...CLOSING THE BUCKLE WOULD SEEM A LOGICAL WAY TO ACTIVATE IT.
STILL, IT SEEMS WE'LL HAVE TO LOOK ELSEWHERE FOR...
WHAT'S THAT FUNNY SMELL...
WHAT IN THE...?
21

GOOD LORD...!
ACID!!
IF YOU'D BEEN WEARING THAT COSTUME...
... I'D BE VERY DEAD NOW...
WITH NOT MUCH LEFT TO BURY...
THEN...
MASTER BRUCE... SOMEONE IS TRYING TO KILL YOU! JUST LIKE THE OTHERS! BUT WHO COULD IT BE? AND WHY?
UNLESS I'M MISTAKEN, ALFRED, THERE ARE A COUPLE OF MORE IMPORTANT QUESTIONS TO BE ANSWERED FIRST...
SUCH AS WHO'S NEXT...
"AND WHERE AND HOW WILL THE KILLER STRIKE?"
WELL, I MUST SAY I HEARD YOU BIG CITY GALS HAD SOME INTERESTIN' WAYS, DARLIN', BUT IS THIS GETUP STRICTLY...
... NECESSARY...?
...N-NO...!
EEEEHH-AGG

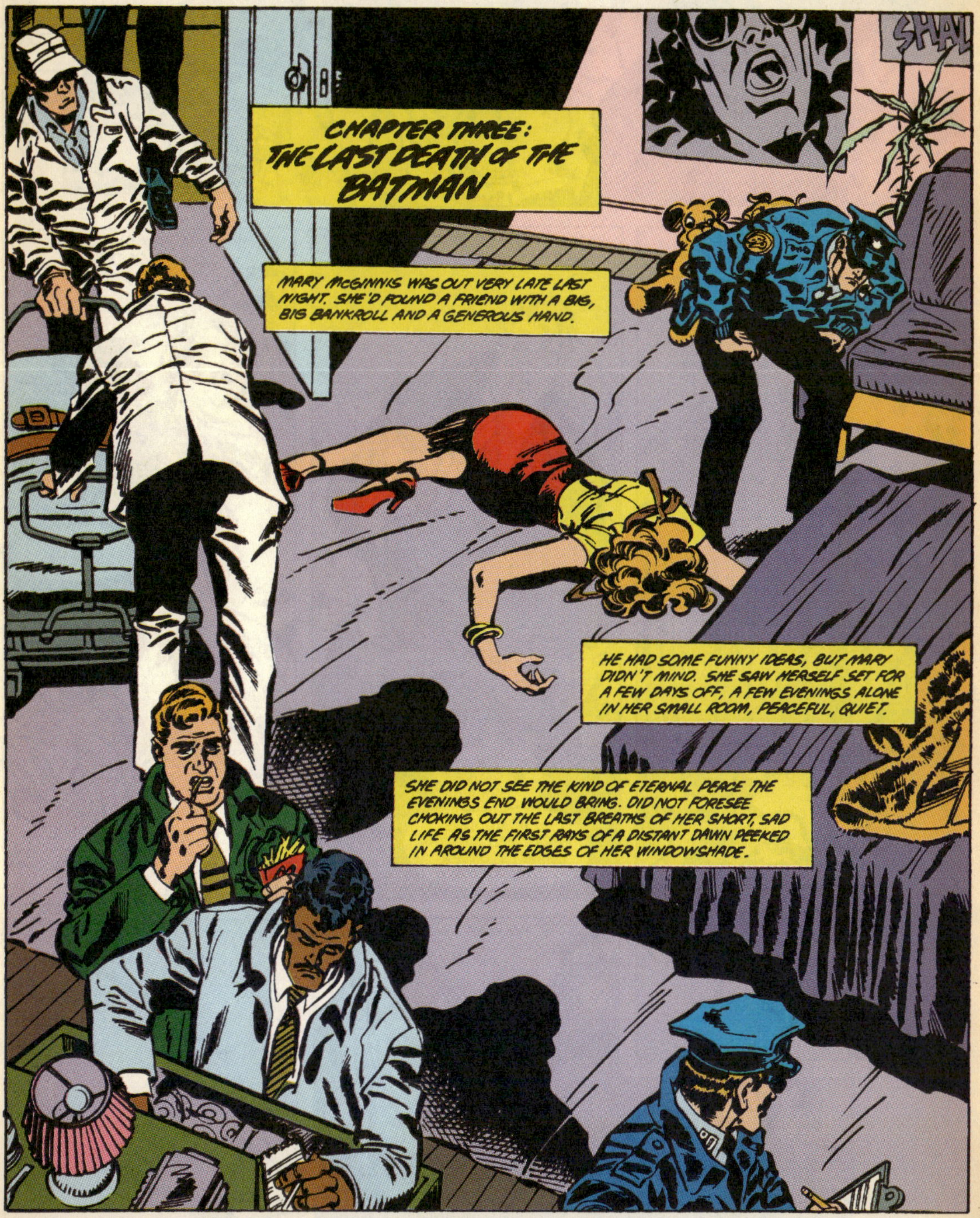
CHAPTER THREE: THE LAST DEATH OF THE BATMAN
MARY McGINNIS WAS OUT VERY LATE LAST NIGHT. SHE'D FOUND A FRIEND WITH A BIG, BIG BANKROLL AND A GENEROUS HAND.
HE HAD SOME FUNNY IDEAS, BUT MARY DIDN'T MIND. SHE SAW HERSELF SET FOR A FEW DAYS OFF, A FEW EVENINGS ALONE IN HER SMALL ROOM, PEACEFUL, QUIET.
SHE DID NOT SEE THE KIND OF ETERNAL PEACE THE EVENINGS END WOULD BRING. DID NOT FORESEE CHOKING OUT THE LAST BREATHS OF HER SHORT, SAD LIFE AS THE FIRST RAYS OF A DISTANT DAWN PEEKED IN AROUND THE EDGES OF HER WINDOWSHADE.

SO WHAT'S THE SCOOP? HOW LONG'S SHE BEEN DEAD?
PARAMEDICS SAY SIX, MAYBE SEVEN HOURS. LUCKY IT'S THE END OF TH' MONTH. COULDA BIN DAYS BEFORE ANYBODY FOUND HER IF THE LANDLADY HADN'T COME POUNDIN' ON TH' DOOR, LOOKIN' FOR HER RENT.
GEEZ...
SHE'S JUST A BABY. MY OWN DAUGHTER'S OLDER.
HEY, INSPECTOR, WHAT DO YOU MAKE OF THIS?
WHATCHA GOT, KID?
I'M NOT SURE, SIR...
SOMETHING SCRATCHED INTO THE CARPET? UNDER HER HAND?
YOU TWO...
GET THIS BED OUT OF THE WAY.
YESSIR, INSPECTOR...
HOL-EEE...!
I'LL BE--
2

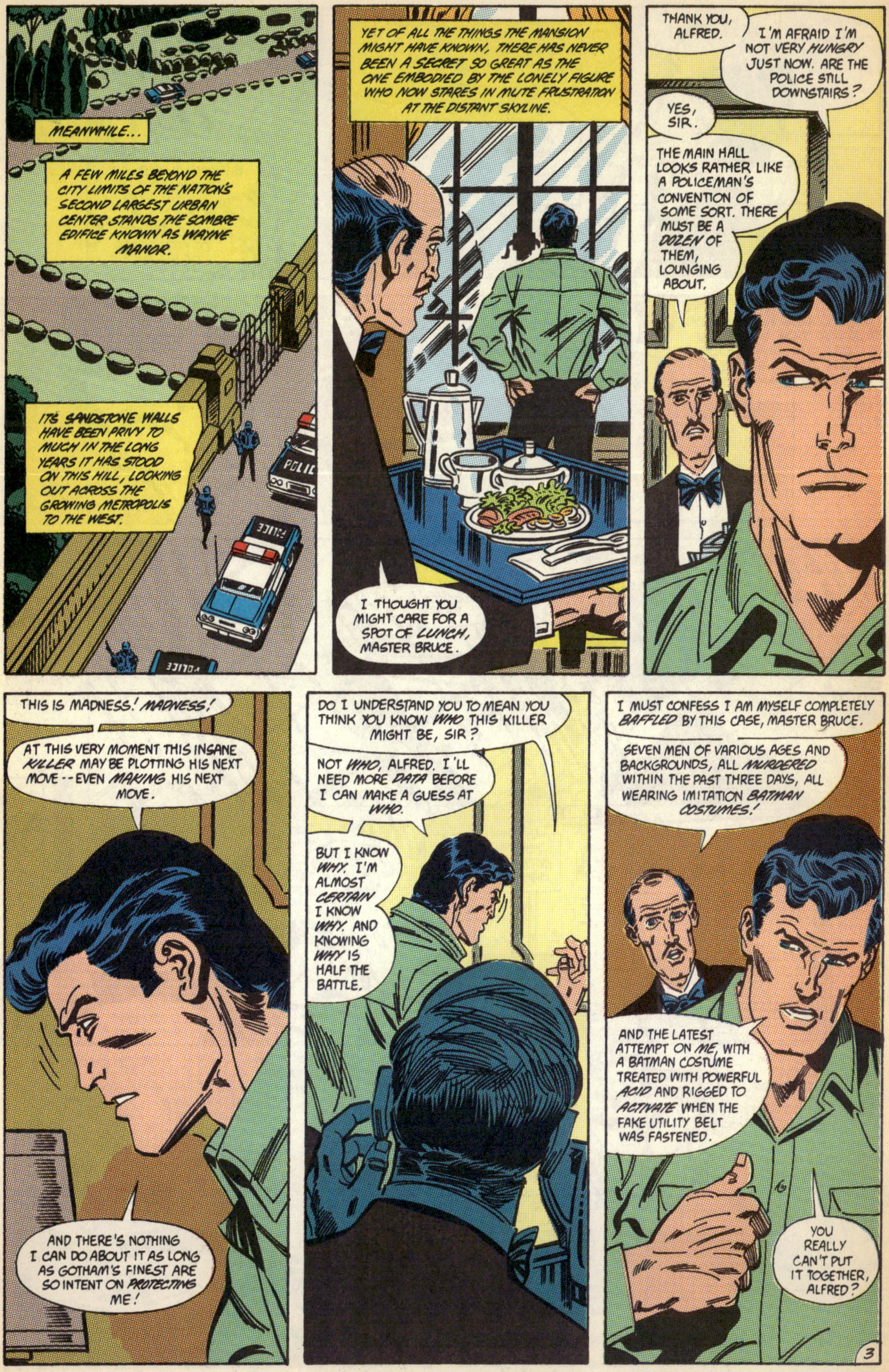
MEANWHILE...
A FEW MILES BEYOND THE CITY LIMITS OF THE NATION'S SECOND LARGEST URBAN CENTER STANDS THE SOMBRE EDIFICE KNOWN AS WAYNE MANOR.
ITS SANDSTONE WALLS HAVE BEEN PRIVY TO MUCH IN THE LONG YEARS IT HAS STOOD ON THIS HILL, LOOKING OUT ACROSS THE GROWING METROPOLIS TO THE WEST.
POLICE
YET OF ALL THE THINGS THE MANSION MIGHT HAVE KNOWN, THERE HAS NEVER BEEN A SECRET SO GREAT AS THE ONE EMBODIED BY THE LONELY FIGURE WHO NOW STARES IN MUTE FRUSTRATION AT THE DISTANT SKYLINE.
I THOUGHT YOU MIGHT CARE FOR A SPOT OF LUNCH, MASTER BRUCE.
THANK YOU, ALFRED.
I'M AFRAID I'M NOT VERY HUNGRY JUST NOW. ARE THE POLICE STILL DOWNSTAIRS?
YES, SIR.
THE MAIN HALL LOOKS RATHER LIKE A POLICEMAN'S CONVENTION OF SOME SORT. THERE MUST BE A DOZEN OF THEM, LOUNGING ABOUT.
THIS IS MADNESS! MADNESS!
AT THIS VERY MOMENT THIS INSANE KILLER MAY BE PLOTTING HIS NEXT MOVE--EVEN MAKING HIS NEXT MOVE.
AND THERE'S NOTHING I CAN DO ABOUT IT AS LONG AS GOTHAM'S FINEST ARE SO INTENT ON PROTECTING ME!
DO I UNDERSTAND YOU TO MEAN YOU THINK YOU KNOW WHO THIS KILLER MIGHT BE, SIR?
NOT WHO, ALFRED. I'LL NEED MORE DATA BEFORE I CAN MAKE A GUESS AT WHO.
BUT I KNOW WHY. I'M ALMOST CERTAIN I KNOW WHY. AND KNOWING WHY IS HALF THE BATTLE.
I MUST CONFESS I AM MYSELF COMPLETELY BAFFLED BY THIS CASE, MASTER BRUCE.
SEVEN MEN OF VARIOUS AGES AND BACKGROUNDS, ALL MURDERED WITHIN THE PAST THREE DAYS, ALL WEARING IMITATION BATMAN COSTUMES!
AND THE LATEST ATTEMPT ON ME, WITH A BATMAN COSTUME TREATED WITH POWERFUL ACID AND RIGGED TO ACTIVATE WHEN THE FAKE UTILITY BELT WAS FASTENED.
YOU REALLY CAN'T PUT IT TOGETHER, ALFRED?

NO, SIR.
IF THE ATTACK HAD BEEN AGAINST YOU *ALONE* I WOULD HAVE SUSPECTED SOMEONE HAD UNCOVERED YOUR *SECRET*...
BUT ALL THESE OTHER GENTLEMEN... SURELY THIS MAD KILLER CANNOT BELIEVE YOU ARE *ALL* THE BATMAN?
NOT THE BATMAN, ALFRED. NOT EXACTLY.
BUT *PIECES* OF HIM. PIECES OF HIS *PAST*.
YOU KNOW ME PROBABLY BETTER THAN ANYONE ELSE ON EARTH, ALFRED. YOU KNOW I'M NEVER ONE TO SING MY OWN PRAISES.
BUT I'LL SAY RIGHT NOW THAT KEEPING A CALM, STRAIGHT FACE AS JIM GORDON READ OFF THE NAMES OF THE MURDERED MEN HAS TO HAVE BEEN ONE OF THE GREATEST *ACTING JOBS* OF ALL TIME!
YOU SEE, I *KNEW* THEM, ALFRED. KNEW EACH AND EVERY ONE OF THEM.
WITHOUT *THEM* THERE MIGHT NEVER HAVE *BEEN* A BATMAN!
MEANWHILE...
THE OFFICE OF GOTHAM'S POLICE COMMISSIONER...
COMMISSIONER GORDON?
DO YOU HAVE A MOMENT?
I SEEM TO HAVE NOTHING *BUT* MOMENTS, DOCTOR.
FRUSTRATING, INCONCLUSIVE MOMENTS THAT WILL NOT FIT THEMSELVES INTO A DECENT CHAIN OF LOGIC.
WHOEVER OUR MYSTERY KILLER IS, HE-- OR SHE-- SEEMS QUITE *DETERMINED* NOT TO LEAVE US THE SLIGHTEST CLUE TO HIS IDENTITY.
THERE'S NOTHING? NOTHING AT ALL?
NOTHING.
LOOK AT THIS, DOCTOR. SEVEN MURDERS. ONE ATTEMPT. AND YET I MIGHT AS WELL BE CHASING A GHOST. WHOEVER IS DOING THIS LEAVES *NO CLUES*. NONE WHATSOEVER.
WELL, I DON'T KNOW IF WHAT I HAVE TO SAY WILL *HELP*, THEN...
...OR JUST MAKE MATTERS WORSE.
4

SPARE ME THE OMINOUS PRONOUNCEMENTS, DOCTOR. WHAT HAVE YOU GOT?
WELL, IT'S THE SECOND BAT-KILLING. STONE, THE DEMOLITIONS EXPERT WHO WAS BLOWN UP ON HIS HOTEL TERRACE.
I JUST GOT FINISHED READING THE DETAILED REPORT ON WHAT WAS LEFT OF THE BODY, AND THERE'S JUST A HINT OF EVIDENCE THAT HE MIGHT HAVE ALREADY BEEN DEAD WHEN HE WAS... EXPLODED.
ALREADY DEAD?
YES, IT'S ODD, TOO. I MEAN, WE DIDN'T HAVE VERY MUCH TO GO ON, BUT...
WELL, IN THE CASE OF ALL THE OTHERS, THE CAUSE OF DEATH WAS JUST WHAT IT APPEARED TO BE. LASALLE WAS BEATEN AND CRUCIFIED. JENNER DROWNED. IF THE ATTEMPT ON BRUCE WAYNE HAD BEEN SUCCESSFUL...
BUT STONE'S BODY--THE PIECES OF IT WE FOUND--HAD BEEN DEAD FOR SEVERAL DAYS WHEN IT WAS EXPLODED.
ALREADY DEAD. ALREADY DEAD.
WHAT DOES THAT MEAN? WHAT COULD IT MEAN?
IS IT POSSIBLE SOME-ONE IS PLAYING A GAME OF "LEAF IN THE FOREST" WITH US?
A... WHAT?
"LEAF IN THE FOREST," DOCTOR.
IT'S AN OLD CONCEPT--TO HIDE A LEAF, YOU PUT IT IN A FOREST, HIDE A PLAYING CARD IN A DECK, HIDE A BOOK IN A LIBRARY...
WHAT WE MAY HAVE HERE IS ONE SPECIFIC VICTIM WHOSE DEATH IS BEING HIDDEN IN THE MIDST OF ALL THESE OTHERS. WHILE WE WASTE TIME SEARCHING FOR A CONNECTION BETWEEN THE MURDERED MEN, THE REAL MOTIVE AND--IF YOU WILL--THE REAL MURDER SLIPS PAST US.
BUT... THE BATMAN COSTUMES?
WINDOW DRESSING?
A NICE, BIZARRE TOUCH TO TAKE US EVEN FURTHER OFF THE PROPER TRAIL. AFTER ALL, WHEN THE FIRST DEAD "BATMAN" WAS DISCOVERED THE WHOLE CITY WENT INTO MOURNING--THOSE WHO WEREN'T CELEBRATING. EITHER WAY IT THREW US ALL OFF BALANCE.
AND WHILE WE WERE RUNNING AROUND FOLLOWING ALL THESE FALSE LEADS...
JEAN...WHO'S IN CHARGE OF THE STONE PART OF THE BAT-KILLING INVESTIGATION? JURGENS?
TELL HIM TO PULL OUT ALL THE STOPS ON THAT ONE. FIND OUT EVERYTHING ABOUT STONE. FRIENDS. ENEMIES. ALL HIS MOVEMENTS AND THEIRS.
WE MAY HAVE FOUND THE PATH TO OUR KILLER...
5

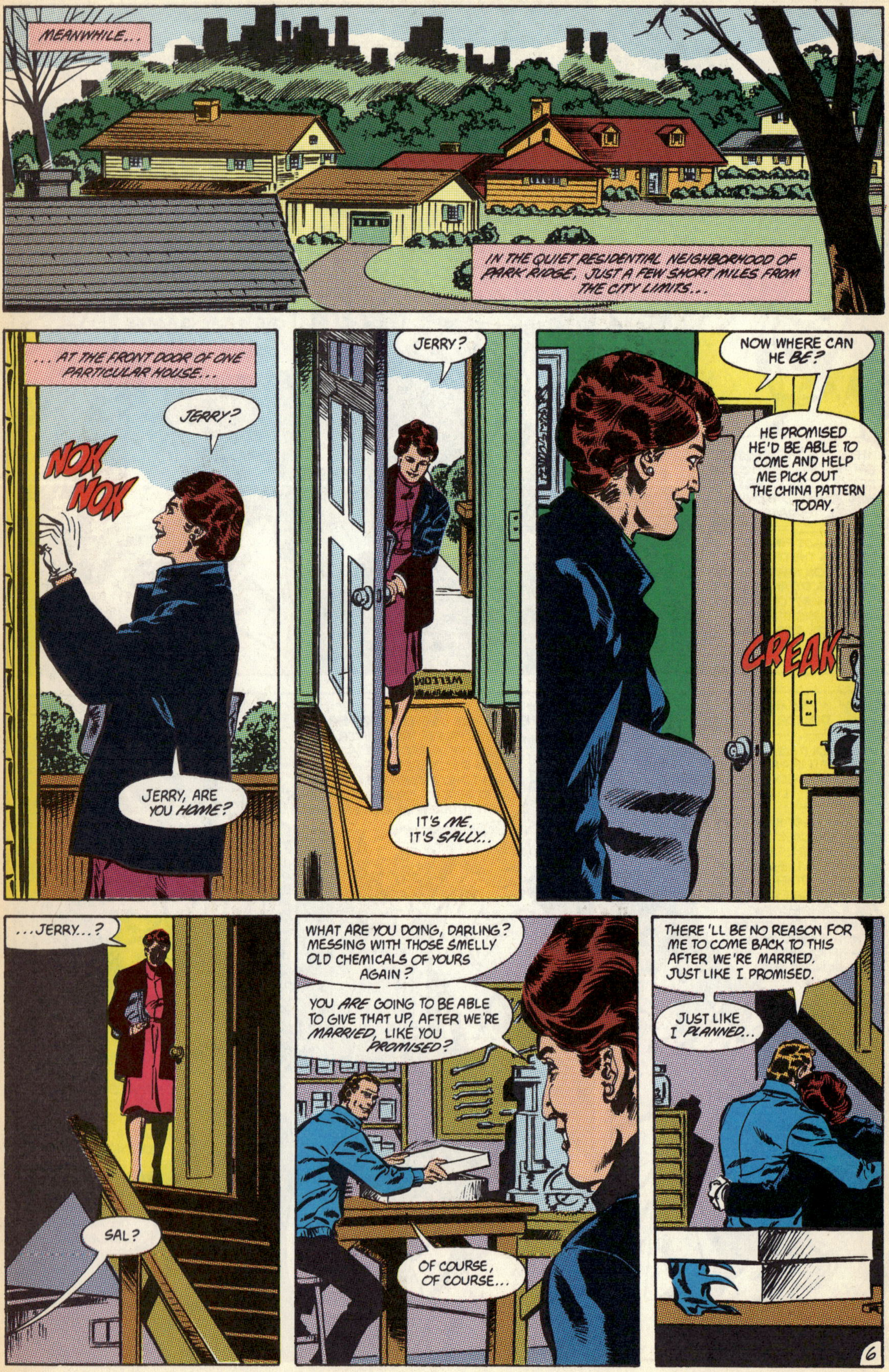
MEANWHILE...
IN THE QUIET RESIDENTIAL NEIGHBORHOOD OF PARK RIDGE, JUST A FEW SHORT MILES FROM THE CITY LIMITS...
...AT THE FRONT DOOR OF ONE PARTICULAR HOUSE...
JERRY?
NOK NOK
JERRY, ARE YOU HOME?
JERRY?
IT'S ME. IT'S SALLY..
NOW WHERE CAN HE BE?
HE PROMISED HE'D BE ABLE TO COME AND HELP ME PICK OUT THE CHINA PATTERN TODAY.
CREAK
...JERRY...?
SAL?
WHAT ARE YOU DOING, DARLING? MESSING WITH THOSE SMELLY OLD CHEMICALS OF YOURS AGAIN?
YOU ARE GOING TO BE ABLE TO GIVE THAT UP, AFTER WE'RE MARRIED, LIKE YOU PROMISED?
OF COURSE, OF COURSE...
THERE'LL BE NO REASON FOR ME TO COME BACK TO THIS AFTER WE'RE MARRIED. JUST LIKE I PROMISED.
JUST LIKE I PLANNED...
6

MEANWHILE...
THIS HAS GONE ON LONG ENOUGH.
I'VE GOT TO GET DOWN TO THE LIBRARY... THE ACCESS TO THE BATCAVE.
WE'RE GOING TO HAVE TO FIND SOMETHING TO DISTRACT THOSE POLICEMEN DOWNSTAIRS.
BUT, WHAT, SIR?
COMMISSIONER GORDON ORDERED THEM TO PROTECT YOU... AND MADE IT QUITE CLEAR ANYONE WHO WAS THE SLIGHTEST BIT DERELICT IN THAT DUTY WOULD FIND HIMSELF WORKING AS A METER MAID...
NEVERTHELESS...
I HAVE TO GET PAST THOSE POLICEMEN. I HAVE TO GET TO THE BATCAVE. THERE ARE LIVES AT RISK. PEOPLE WHO NEED MY PROTECTION.
NOT EVEN MY SECRET IDENTITY IS SUFFICIENTLY VALUABLE THAT I CAN RISK MORE DEATHS JUST TO PRESERVE IT.
IF IT COMES DOWN TO IT, I'M GOING TO WALK RIGHT PAST THOSE POLICEMEN, AND THEY CAN FOLLOW ME TO THE BATCAVE IF THEY HAVE TO!
I'M SURE THAT WILL NOT BE NECESSARY, SIR.
I BELIEVE THERE IS SOMETHING I CAN DO. JUST GIVE ME FIFTEEN MINUTES.
ALL RIGHT, ALFRED. BUT NOT ONE SECOND LONGER...
"THERE'S TOO MUCH AT STAKE..."
OH DEAR, OH DEAR...
IT'S BEEN A LONG TIME SINCE I'VE SEEN MASTER BRUCE IN SUCH A STATE!

I ONLY HOPE THIS WORKS.
I WAS PLANNING TO SERVE THIS ROAST FOR SUNDAY DINNER...
I HAVEN'T USED THIS MICROWAVE OVEN MORE THAN TWICE IN THE THREE YEARS WE'VE HAD THE WRETCHED THING...
I CERTAINLY NEVER EXPECTED TO BE USING IT TO DESTROY SUCH A SPLENDID CUT OF LAMB...
BEEP
BEEP
BEEP
ELEVEN MINUTES LATER...
MAN O MAN, WHAT IS THAT SMELL?
MY MOUTH'S WATERIN' ENOUGH T'DROWN ME!
GOOD AFTERNOON, OFFICERS.
I WONDER IF I MIGHT OFFER YOU A SPOT OF LUNCH?
HEY, YOU DON'T HAVE TO ASK ME TWICE!
WHATCHA COOKIN', PAL? SMELLS DELICIOSO!
HEY, HOLD IT! ARE YOU GUYS CRAZY?
GORDON'LL HAVE US ROASTED IF WE LEAVE...
I'M NOT SUGGESTING YOU LEAVE, OFFICER. MERELY TRANSFER YOUR GUARD POSTS TO THE KITCHEN.
YEAH...
C'MON, MORRIE, IT'S NOT LIKE WE'RE RUNNIN' OFF T' McDONALD'S OR SOMETHIN'.
I DUNNO...
YEAH! COME ON, MORRIE!
MAY I REMIND YOU OF YOUR COMPATRIOTS OUTSIDE?
I DOUBT THAT ANYONE WILL BE ABLE TO REACH THE HOUSE WITH THEM PATROLLING THE GROUNDS.
BRILLIANT, OLD FRIEND.
BRILLIANT.

THREE MINUTES LATER, FAR BELOW WAYNE MANOR...
NONE OF THE MURDER VICTIMS WERE GOTHAM NATIVES.
WHOEVER IT IS THAT'S KILLING THEM MUST ALSO HAVE BEEN BRINGING THEM INTO TOWN...
LURING THEM SOMEHOW.
WITH MY COMPUTER LINKS TO ALL THE MAJOR SYSTEMS IN GOTHAM I CAN EASILY TAP INTO THE VARIOUS TRAIN, BUS AND AIRLINE SCHEDULES...
AND PASSENGER LISTS.
TENS OF THOUSANDS OF PEOPLE COME INTO GOTHAM EVERY DAY.
FINDING A NEEDLE IN A HAYSTACK WOULD BE CHILD'S PLAY COMPARED TO THIS...
...IF I DIDN'T HAVE THE DISTINCT ADVANTAGE OF KNOWING EXACTLY WHICH NAMES I'M LOOKING FOR.
THIRTY FOUR MINUTES LATER...
THE SANDBERG HOTEL...
THIS IS BOCH'S ROOM.
DOESN'T LOOK LIKE HE'S HERE. IF I'M TOO LATE...

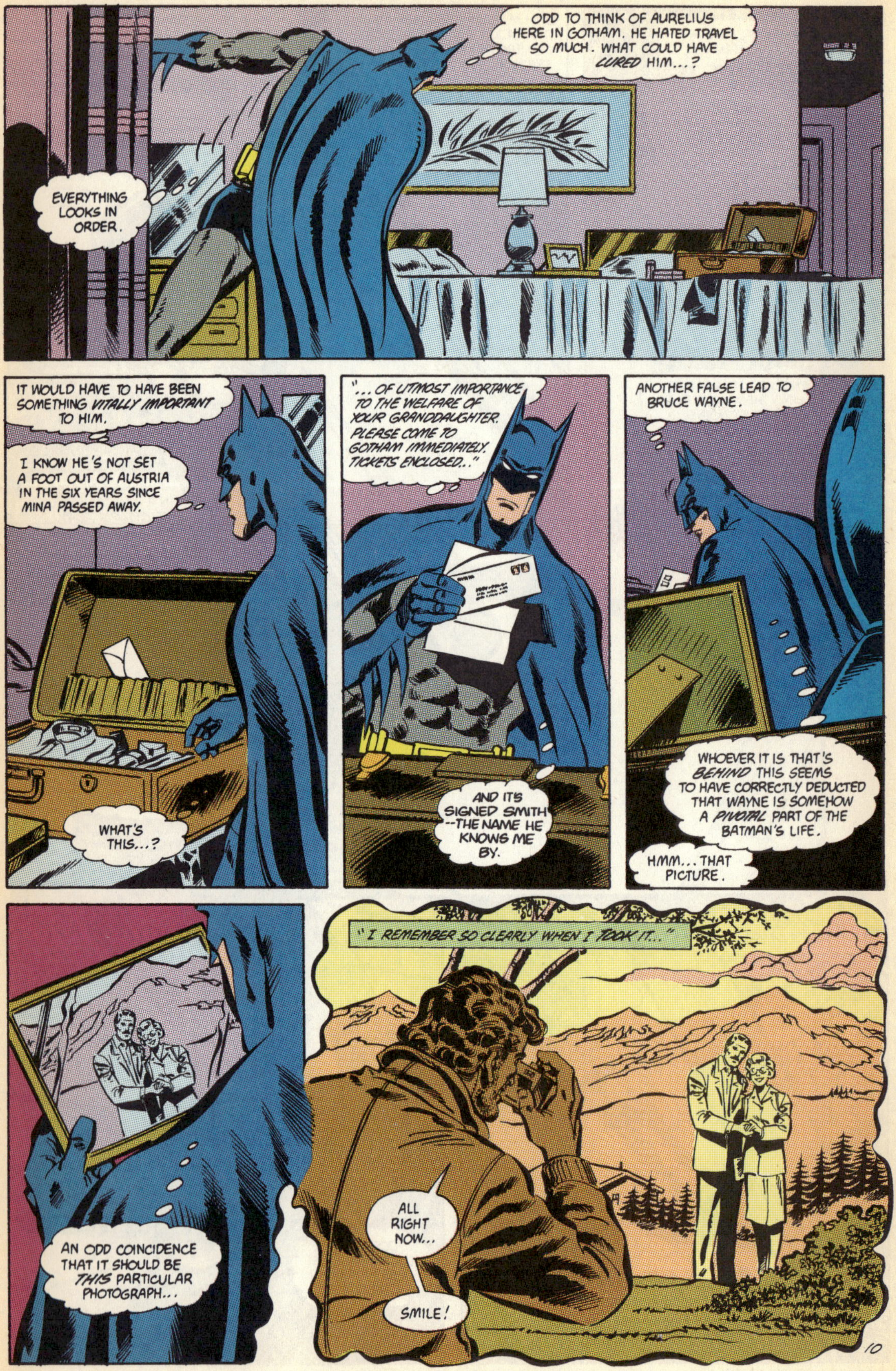
ODD TO THINK OF AURELIUS HERE IN GOTHAM. HE HATED TRAVEL SO MUCH. WHAT COULD HAVE LURED HIM...?
EVERYTHING LOOKS IN ORDER.
IT WOULD HAVE TO HAVE BEEN SOMETHING VITALLY IMPORTANT TO HIM.
I KNOW HE'S NOT SET A FOOT OUT OF AUSTRIA IN THE SIX YEARS SINCE MINA PASSED AWAY.
WHAT'S THIS...?
"...OF UTMOST IMPORTANCE TO THE WELFARE OF YOUR GRANDDAUGHTER. PLEASE COME TO GOTHAM IMMEDIATELY. TICKETS ENCLOSED..."
AND IT'S SIGNED SMITH --THE NAME HE KNOWS ME BY.
ANOTHER FALSE LEAD TO BRUCE WAYNE.
WHOEVER IT IS THAT'S BEHIND THIS SEEMS TO HAVE CORRECTLY DEDUCTED THAT WAYNE IS SOMEHOW A PIVOTAL PART OF THE BATMAN'S LIFE.
HMM...THAT PICTURE.
AN ODD COINCIDENCE THAT IT SHOULD BE THIS PARTICULAR PHOTOGRAPH...
"I REMEMBER SO CLEARLY WHEN I TOOK IT..."
ALL RIGHT NOW...
SMILE!
10

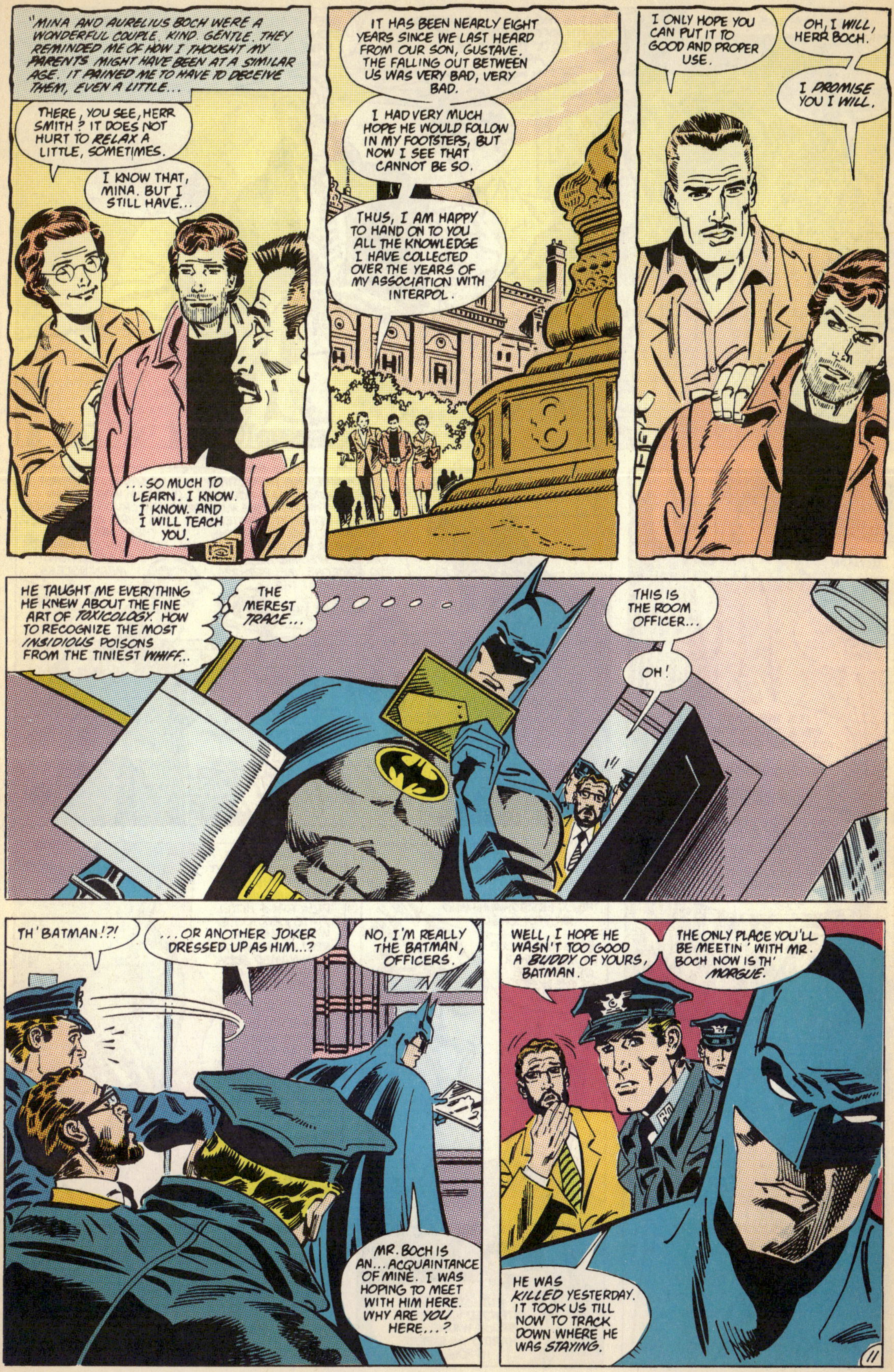
"MINA AND AURELIUS BOCH WERE A WONDERFUL COUPLE. KIND. GENTLE. THEY REMINDED ME OF HOW I THOUGHT MY PARENTS MIGHT HAVE BEEN AT A SIMILAR AGE. IT PAINED ME TO HAVE TO DECEIVE THEM, EVEN A LITTLE...
THERE, YOU SEE, HERR SMITH? IT DOES NOT HURT TO RELAX A LITTLE, SOMETIMES.
I KNOW THAT, MINA. BUT I STILL HAVE...
...SO MUCH TO LEARN. I KNOW. I KNOW. AND I WILL TEACH YOU.
IT HAS BEEN NEARLY EIGHT YEARS SINCE WE LAST HEARD FROM OUR SON, GUSTAVE. THE FALLING OUT BETWEEN US WAS VERY BAD, VERY BAD.
I HAD VERY MUCH HOPE HE WOULD FOLLOW IN MY FOOTSTEPS, BUT NOW I SEE THAT CANNOT BE SO.
THUS, I AM HAPPY TO HAND ON TO YOU ALL THE KNOWLEDGE I HAVE COLLECTED OVER THE YEARS OF MY ASSOCIATION WITH INTERPOL.
I ONLY HOPE YOU CAN PUT IT TO GOOD AND PROPER USE.
OH, I WILL, HERR BOCH.
I PROMISE YOU I WILL.
HE TAUGHT ME EVERYTHING HE KNEW ABOUT THE FINE ART OF TOXICOLOGY. HOW TO RECOGNIZE THE MOST INSIDIOUS POISONS FROM THE TINIEST WHIFF..
THE MEREST TRACE...
THIS IS THE ROOM OFFICER...
OH!
TH' BATMAN!?!
...OR ANOTHER JOKER DRESSED UP AS HIM...?
NO, I'M REALLY THE BATMAN, OFFICERS.
MR. BOCH IS AN...ACQUAINTANCE OF MINE. I WAS HOPING TO MEET WITH HIM HERE. WHY ARE YOU HERE...?
WELL, I HOPE HE WASN'T TOO GOOD A BUDDY OF YOURS, BATMAN.
THE ONLY PLACE YOU'LL BE MEETIN' WITH MR. BOCH NOW IS TH' MORGUE.
HE WAS KILLED YESTERDAY. IT TOOK US TILL NOW TO TRACK DOWN WHERE HE WAS STAYING.

POLICE MORGUE, LATER...
THIS IS THE LAST ONE. WEBBER. DEATH BY SNAKEBITE. I DON'T EVEN HAVE TO DO THE AUTOPSY. THE SIGNS ARE PLAIN.
THEN IT ALL COMES BACK TO STONE, TO THE ONE WHO MAY HAVE ALREADY BEEN DEAD...
OR WHO MAY NOT HAVE BEEN STONE.
BATMAN!
WHAT DO YOU MEAN... "NOT STONE?"
IT'S THE OTHER PIECE THAT DOESN'T MATCH THE SHAPE OF THE REST OF THE PUZZLE, COMMISSIONER.
IN ADDITION TO BEING ALREADY DEAD AT THE TIME-- YES, I'VE READ YOUR REPORT, DOCTOR--STONE WAS THE ONLY ONE KILLED IN THE MANNER OF HIS EXPERTISE.
CONSIDERING THE VICTIMS CHRONOLOGICALLY, ROUGHLY HALFWAY THROUGH THIS MURDER SPREE A DELIBERATE PATTERN BEGINS TO EVOLVE, AS IF THE MURDERER HAS DECIDED TO SEND A SPECIFIC MESSAGE TO SOMEONE. ME, PERHAPS, THOUGH WHAT THE MESSAGE IS ELUDES ME.
LA SALLE, THE FIRST VICTIM, WAS BEATEN AND CRUCIFIED. JENNER, THE THIRD, WAS DROWNED. THESE ARE APPARENTLY RANDOM METHODS OF EXECUTION, MEANINGLESS.
BUT ALLISON, THE GYMNAST, WAS SHOT WITH A RIGGED CROSSBOW. HIS DEATH WAS FOLLOWED BY DIGIORDA'S, THE EXPERT BOWMAN WHO WAS POISONED...
EACH WAS KILLED IN THE MANNER OF EXPERTISE OF THE NEXT VICTIM.
BUT... THE NEXT INTENDED VICTIM WAS BRUCE WAYNE. HE'S HARDLY AN EXPERT IN POISONS.
NO. HOWEVER, HE WAS NOT THE NEXT VICTIM. THE CLUE YOU FOUND IN DIGIORDA'S HOTEL SUITE LED YOU TO WAYNE, BUT THE NEXT VICTIM WAS A MAN NAMED BOCH. AN EXPERT ON ALL FORMS OF POISON.
HE WAS KILLED BY AN ARMORED CAR PAINTED WITH THE WAYNE FOUNDATION LOGO... ANOTHER RATHER CLUMSY CONNECTION TO BRUCE WAYNE.
BUT PERHAPS THE ONLY ONE WHICH COULD MAKE THIS NEW "PATTERN" WORK TO INCLUDE WAYNE.
12

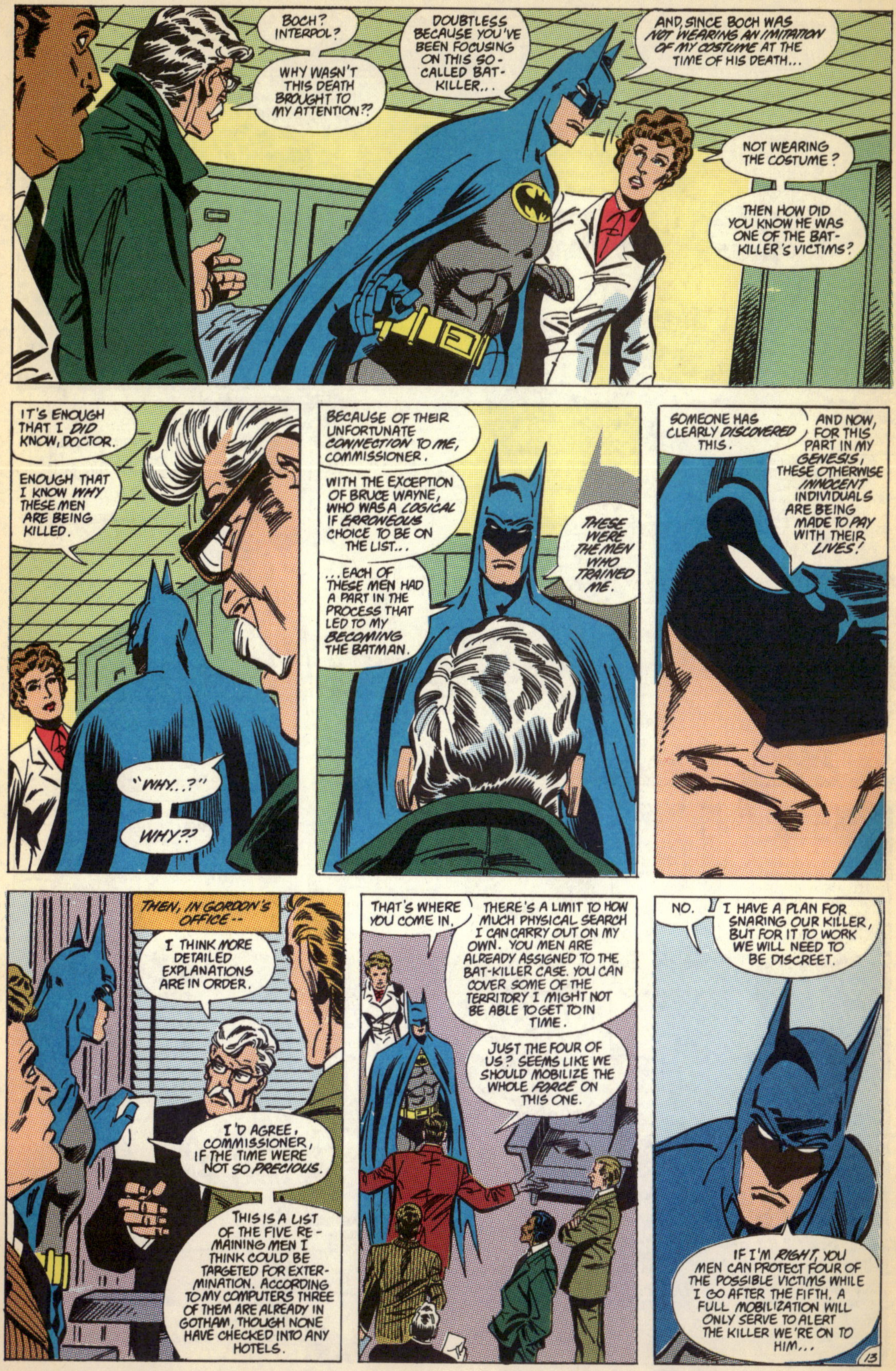
BOCH? INTERPOL?
WHY WASN'T THIS DEATH BROUGHT TO MY ATTENTION??
DOUBTLESS BECAUSE YOU'VE BEEN FOCUSING ON THIS SO-CALLED BAT-KILLER...
AND, SINCE BOCH WAS NOT WEARING AN IMITATION OF MY COSTUME AT THE TIME OF HIS DEATH...
NOT WEARING THE COSTUME?
THEN HOW DID YOU KNOW HE WAS ONE OF THE BAT-KILLER'S VICTIMS?
IT'S ENOUGH THAT I DID KNOW, DOCTOR.
ENOUGH THAT I KNOW WHY THESE MEN ARE BEING KILLED.
"WHY..?"
WHY??
BECAUSE OF THEIR UNFORTUNATE CONNECTION TO ME, COMMISSIONER.
WITH THE EXCEPTION OF BRUCE WAYNE, WHO WAS A LOGICAL IF ERRONEOUS CHOICE TO BE ON THE LIST...
...EACH OF THESE MEN HAD A PART IN THE PROCESS THAT LED TO MY BECOMING THE BATMAN.
THESE WERE THE MEN WHO TRAINED ME.
SOMEONE HAS CLEARLY DISCOVERED THIS.
AND NOW, FOR THIS PART IN MY GENESIS, THESE OTHERWISE INNOCENT INDIVIDUALS ARE BEING MADE TO PAY WITH THEIR LIVES!
THEN, IN GORDON'S OFFICE--
I THINK MORE DETAILED EXPLANATIONS ARE IN ORDER.
I'D AGREE, COMMISSIONER, IF THE TIME WERE NOT SO PRECIOUS.
THIS IS A LIST OF THE FIVE RE-MAINING MEN I THINK COULD BE TARGETED FOR EXTER-MINATION. ACCORDING TO MY COMPUTERS THREE OF THEM ARE ALREADY IN GOTHAM, THOUGH NONE HAVE CHECKED INTO ANY HOTELS.
THAT'S WHERE YOU COME IN.
THERE'S A LIMIT TO HOW MUCH PHYSICAL SEARCH I CAN CARRY OUT ON MY OWN. YOU MEN ARE ALREADY ASSIGNED TO THE BAT-KILLER CASE. YOU CAN COVER SOME OF THE TERRITORY I MIGHT NOT BE ABLE TO GET TO IN TIME.
JUST THE FOUR OF US? SEEMS LIKE WE SHOULD MOBILIZE THE WHOLE FORCE ON THIS ONE.
NO.
I HAVE A PLAN FOR SNARING OUR KILLER, BUT FOR IT TO WORK WE WILL NEED TO BE DISCREET.
IF I'M RIGHT, YOU MEN CAN PROTECT FOUR OF THE POSSIBLE VICTIMS WHILE I GO AFTER THE FIFTH. A FULL MOBILIZATION WILL ONLY SERVE TO ALERT THE KILLER WE'RE ON TO HIM...
13

"IF THAT HAPPENS, I'M AFRAID WE'LL LOSE HIM FOREVER..."
SEVERAL HOURS LATER...
WHERE IS IT?
WHERE'S 1307...?
THERE IT IS...
AND THERE HE IS.
MR. SHASTRI! GLAD YOU COULD MAKE IT, SIR.
MR. JONES...
I KNOW YOU'RE A VERY BUSY MAN, SIR. I'M SO PLEASED YOU COULD TAKE A MOMENT FROM YOUR SCHEDULE.
Trade Winds IMPORT AND EXPORT INC.
SINCE WE COULD AGREE TO MEET HERE, AT ONE OF MY HOLDINGS, I AM ABLE TO COMBINE MY BUSINESS WITH YOURS. THEREFORE I AM SATISFIED.
SHALL WE STEP INSIDE?
NOW, MR. JONES, PERHAPS YOU WILL TELL ME WHAT THIS IS ALL ABOUT? YOUR COMMUNICATION WITH MY DELHI OFFICE WAS MOST MYSTERIOUS.
I REALIZE THAT, SIR.
IT WAS NECESSARY THAT I NOT REVEAL ALL THE DETAILS IN MY CABLE. YOU SEE...
I AM THE BATMAN.. AND I NEED YOUR HELP.
YOU ARE THE BATMAN?
FORGIVE ME, MR. JONES, BUT YOU DO NOT SEEM TO POSSESS THE NECESSARY PHYSIQUE...
I AM A MASTER OF DISGUISE, SIR.
PERHAPS IT WOULD HELP YOU BELIEVE ME IF I REMIND YOU OF THE YOUNG AMERI-CAN WITH WHOM YOU ONCE SHARED YOUR GREAT KNOWLEDGE OF OPHIDIA..?
IT IS TRUE I HAVE BEEN ACKNOWLEDGED AS THE WORLD'S LEADING EXPERT ON THE SUBJECT OF SNAKES, MR. JONES. EVEN AS MY BUSINESS ASSUMED WORLDWIDE PROPORTIONS, THIS HAS REMAINED AN ABIDING INTEREST.
BUT I AM AFRAID YOU ARE MISTAKEN. I HAVE NEVER TUTORED AN AMERICAN.
NEVER..??
BUT... I WAS SO SURE... THE TIME...
14

DOES... DOES THAT MEAN...
DOES THAT MEAN... YOU WON'T... HELP ME?
I THINK THAT MEANS YOU'RE BEYOND HELP, STONE.
NOW, WHY DON'T YOU SURRENDER QUIETLY...
THAT VOICE!
YOU'RE NOT SHASTRI!
NO, STONE.
BUT AS YOU SAID, A MASTER OF DISGUISE...
BATMAN!
THE REAL ONE!
STONE!
SKZZKZZT
AH-GHH!!
STONE! STOP! IT'S POINTLESS TO RUN! I KNOW WHO YOU ARE!
NO YOU DON'T, BATMAN.
"STONE" IS DEAD. I KILLED HIM! ALL THE TRAILS THAT LEAD TO HIM END WITH THE NAMELESS CADAVER I EXPLODED OVER DOWNTOWN GOTHAM. THE CADAVER I DRESSED AS YOU... TO MATCH THE PATTERN... TO MAKE SURE EVERYONE THOUGHT I WAS DEAD!
DON'T... TRY TO KID YOURSELF, STONE.
NO ONE CAN VANISH SO COMPLETELY I'D NEVER BE ABLE TO FIND THEM.
I HAVE, BATMAN.
DON'T YOU SEE? THAT'S WHERE I BEGAN. THAT WAS THE CORE OF MY WHOLE PLAN.
I'VE SPENT YEARS CREATING A WHOLE NEW LIFE, BATMAN. AND NOT YOU, NOR ANY OF YOUR ENEMIES ARE EVER GOING TO HARM US!
"...US...?"
15

ONE HOUR LATER...
BUT, MASTER BRUCE, IF YOU KNOW THIS MAN STONE IS THE KILLER, WHY DON'T YOU JUST GO OUT AND PICK HIM UP?
BECAUSE HE WAS TELLING THE TRUTH, ALFRED.
ALL DATA ON FREDRICK STONE ENDS WITH HIS APPARENT DEATH.
BUT IF MR. STONE IS ONE OF THE MEN YOU CONTACTED, YEARS AGO, TO HELP YOU IN YOUR TRAINING...
WHY WOULD HE BE KILLING OFF ALL THE OTHERS WHO HELPED TO THAT SAME END... INCLUDING HIMSELF? AND WHY WOULD BRUCE WAYNE BE ON HIS LIST OF VICTIMS?
I'M NOT SURE WHAT HIS EXACT MOTIVE IS JUST YET.
AS TO HIS INCLUSION OF BRUCE WAYNE, I SUSPECT THAT WAS A RESULT OF HIS PROCESS OF DEDUCTION IN FINDING ALL THE OTHERS.
I LEARNED ABOUT EXPLOSIVES FROM STONE.
HE MUST'VE READ OF MY USING A METHOD ONLY HE COULD HAVE TAUGHT ME. AND FROM THAT, HE REASONED OTHER EXPERTS MUST HAVE TAUGHT ME OTHER SKILLS.
AS FOR BRUCE WAYNE... WELL, RA'S AL GHUL ONCE DEDUCED MY IDENTITY BY LOCATING THE ONE MAN WHO WAS BUYING ALL THE THINGS BATMAN WOULD NEED.
STONE COULD HAVE MADE A SIMILAR DEDUCTION. PERHAPS HE DECIDED WAYNE WAS SOMEHOW FINANCING THE BATMAN.
WHEN STONE WAS THROWN BY MY PRETENDING SHASTRI WAS NOT ONE OF THE MEN WHO'D TRAINED ME, I REALIZED HE WAS WORKING ON GUESSWORK RATHER THAN DEDUCTIVE REASONING.
IT'S MOST FORTUNATE YOU WERE ABLE TO CONTACT MR. SHASTRI AND TAKE HIS PLACE, SIR.
LUCKILY THE HEAVY LATEX MAKEUP I NEEDED FOR MY IMPERSONATION PROTECTED ME FROM THE ELECTRIC SHOCK THAT WAS MEANT TO KILL SHASTRI.
I WOULD HARDLY SAY THOSE BURNS REPRESENT AN INDICATION OF YOUR HAVING BEEN PROTECTED, MASTER BRUCE.
YOU REALLY SHOULD TRY TO AVOID ANY STRENUOUS ACTIVITY FOR A FEW DAYS.
STONE ISN'T LIKELY TO GIVE ME EVEN A FEW HOURS NOW. NOT KNOWING THAT I KNOW WHO HE IS.
"EVEN IF I DON'T HAVE A CLUE AS TO WHERE HE IS..."
BUT... BUT JERRY, I DON'T UNDERSTAND.
WHAT'S WRONG? WHAT HAPPENED AFTER YOU DROPPED ME OFF DOWNTOWN?
16

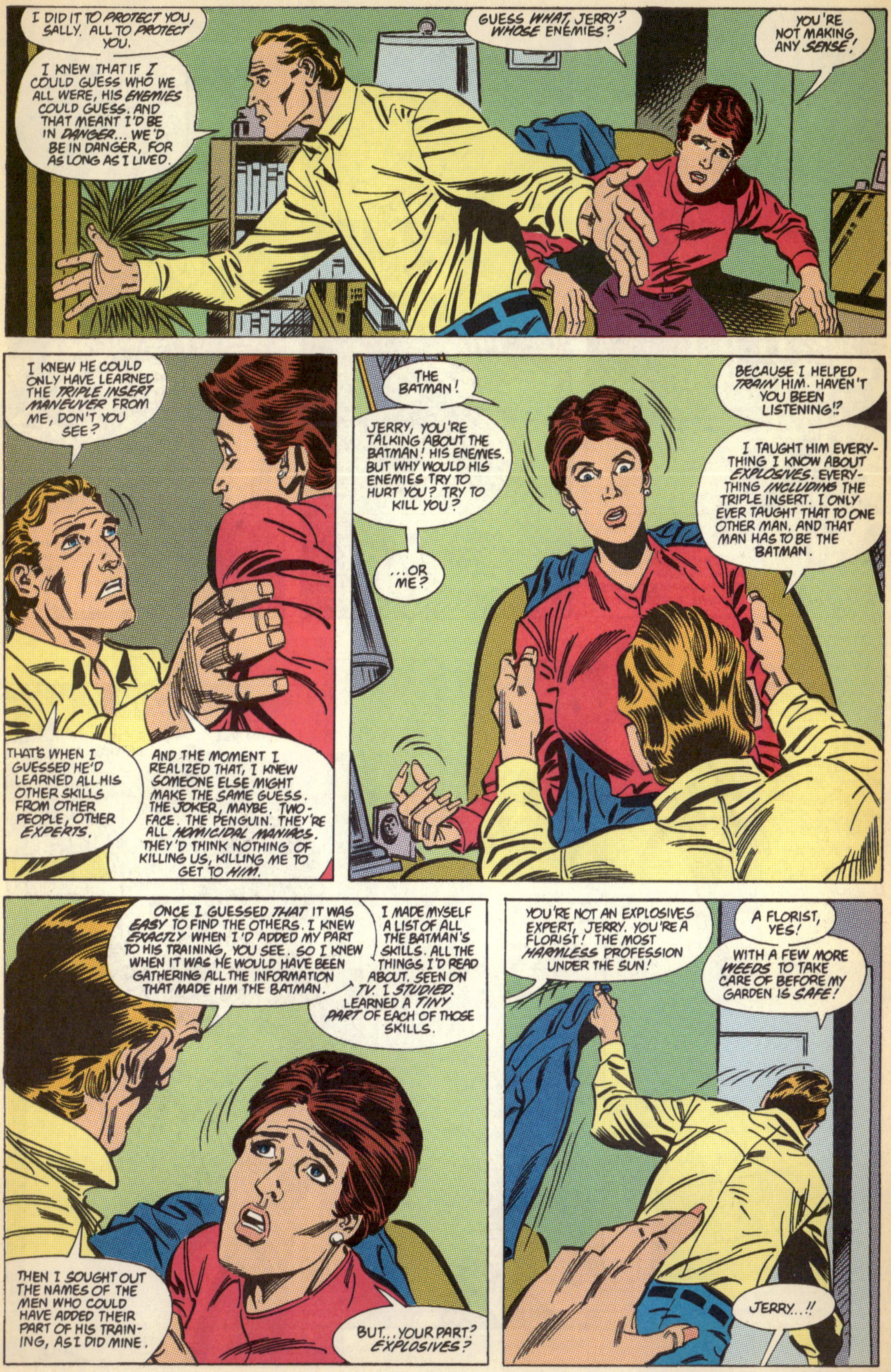
I DID IT TO PROTECT YOU, SALLY. ALL TO PROTECT YOU.
I KNEW THAT IF I COULD GUESS WHO WE ALL WERE, HIS ENEMIES COULD GUESS. AND THAT MEANT I'D BE IN DANGER... WE'D BE IN DANGER, FOR AS LONG AS I LIVED.
GUESS WHAT, JERRY? WHOSE ENEMIES?
YOU'RE NOT MAKING ANY SENSE!
I KNEW HE COULD ONLY HAVE LEARNED THE TRIPLE INSERT MANEUVER FROM ME, DON'T YOU SEE?
THAT'S WHEN I GUESSED HE'D LEARNED ALL HIS OTHER SKILLS FROM OTHER PEOPLE, OTHER EXPERTS.
AND THE MOMENT I REALIZED THAT, I KNEW SOMEONE ELSE MIGHT MAKE THE SAME GUESS. THE JOKER, MAYBE. TWO-FACE. THE PENGUIN. THEY'RE ALL HOMICIDAL MANIACS. THEY'D THINK NOTHING OF KILLING US, KILLING ME TO GET TO HIM.
THE BATMAN!
JERRY, YOU'RE TALKING ABOUT THE BATMAN! HIS ENEMIES. BUT WHY WOULD HIS ENEMIES TRY TO HURT YOU? TRY TO KILL YOU?
...OR ME?
BECAUSE I HELPED TRAIN HIM. HAVEN'T YOU BEEN LISTENING!?
I TAUGHT HIM EVERYTHING I KNOW ABOUT EXPLOSIVES. EVERYTHING INCLUDING THE TRIPLE INSERT. I ONLY EVER TAUGHT THAT TO ONE OTHER MAN. AND THAT MAN HAS TO BE THE BATMAN.
ONCE I GUESSED THAT IT WAS EASY TO FIND THE OTHERS. I KNEW EXACTLY WHEN I'D ADDED MY PART TO HIS TRAINING, YOU SEE. SO I KNEW WHEN IT WAS HE WOULD HAVE BEEN GATHERING ALL THE INFORMATION THAT MADE HIM THE BATMAN.
I MADE MYSELF A LIST OF ALL THE BATMAN'S SKILLS. ALL THE THINGS I'D READ ABOUT. SEEN ON TV. I STUDIED. LEARNED A TINY PART OF EACH OF THOSE SKILLS.
THEN I SOUGHT OUT THE NAMES OF THE MEN WHO COULD HAVE ADDED THEIR PART OF HIS TRAINING, AS I DID MINE.
BUT... YOUR PART? EXPLOSIVES?
YOU'RE NOT AN EXPLOSIVES EXPERT, JERRY. YOU'RE A FLORIST! THE MOST HARMLESS PROFESSION UNDER THE SUN!
A FLORIST, YES!
WITH A FEW MORE WEEDS TO TAKE CARE OF BEFORE MY GARDEN IS SAFE!
JERRY...!!

WAIT HERE, MY DARLING!
YOU'LL BE SAFE HERE.
IT'S HIM ALL RIGHT... STONE... HIDING IN PLAIN SIGHT UNDER AN ASSUMED NAME, A MANUFACTURED IDENTITY...
JERRY.. PLEASE...
NO...
DON'T WORRY, MISS... I'LL STOP HIM...
OH... OH... M-MY... G-GOD...
DON'T BE AFRAID.
BUT I WOULD SUGGEST YOU LEAVE HERE. IF YOU STAY NOW YOU WILL ONLY INCRIMINATE YOURSELF.
TWENTY MINUTES LATER, THE BRIARCLIFFE ARMS...
I MUST ACT QUICKLY IF THE BATMAN KNOWS WHO I AM HE WILL SURELY ALSO KNOW WHO I'M AFTER.
BUT THERE ARE MORE THAN ONE LEFT TO KILL. HE WILL NOT KNOW WHO IS TO BE NEXT.
ONLY I KNOW THAT.
AND WHATEVER ELSE HIS SKILLS MIGHT BE, THE BATMAN IS NOT A MINDREADER!
MR. CAMPBELL?
ROOM SERVICE...
KNOK KNOK

12
ROOM SERVICE?
I DIDN'T ORDER ANY...
SHUT UP!
I DON'T HAVE THE TIME FOR FINESSE. NO TIME FOR GAMES.
WHOUF!!
YOU'RE GOING TO DIE, CAMPBELL. THAT'S WHY YOU CAME TO GOTHAM, ALTHOUGH YOU HAD NO IDEA WHEN YOU RESPONDED TO MY INVITATION.
AND BEFORE YOU DIE YOU'RE GOING TO PUT THIS ON!
WHAT IN THE NAME OF...??
THE COSTUME IS MY SIGNATURE, CAMPBELL. THE MARK I CHOSE TO LET THE BATMAN'S ENEMIES KNOW WHY THIS WAS BEING DONE. WHY THESE MEN WERE DYING.
YOU HAVE TO DIE SO I CAN LIVE.
PUT IT ON--
SOON--
ALL RIGHT! I'M WEARING THE WRETCHED THING! NOW, WHAT DO YOU MEAN TO DO?
YOU SEE THIS DAGGER, CAMPBELL? IT'S AN EXACT COPY OF A CEREMONIAL DAGGER USED BY THE CHAWALDRA PEOPLES OF NORTHERN TIBET.
IT USED TO BE USED IN HUMAN SACRIFICES, BUT THEY'VE BECOME MORE CIVILIZED IN THE PAST FEW YEARS.
PLEASE... NO... I HAVE A WIFE...
THERE ARE PROBABLY ONLY TWO AMERICANS WHO WOULD RECOGNIZE THIS DAGGER ON SIGHT, CAMPBELL, MY NEXT VICTIM, AND...
...AND ME.

YES, STONE... OR WOULD YOU PREFER "SAWYER"? YOU WENT TO A LOT OF TROUBLE TO CREATE THAT IDENTITY..
BUT IT WON'T SERVE YOU NOW. YOUR SO-CALLED SIGNATURE WAS MEANT TO FOOL MY ENEMIES INTO THINKING ALL THE MEN WHO TRAINED ME WERE DEAD WHEN CORPSES WEARING MY COSTUME STOPPED TURNING UP.
YOU WANTED EVERYONE THINKING YOU WERE GONE. NO LONGER ANY SORT OF TARGET FOR VENGEANCE BY MY ENEMIES.

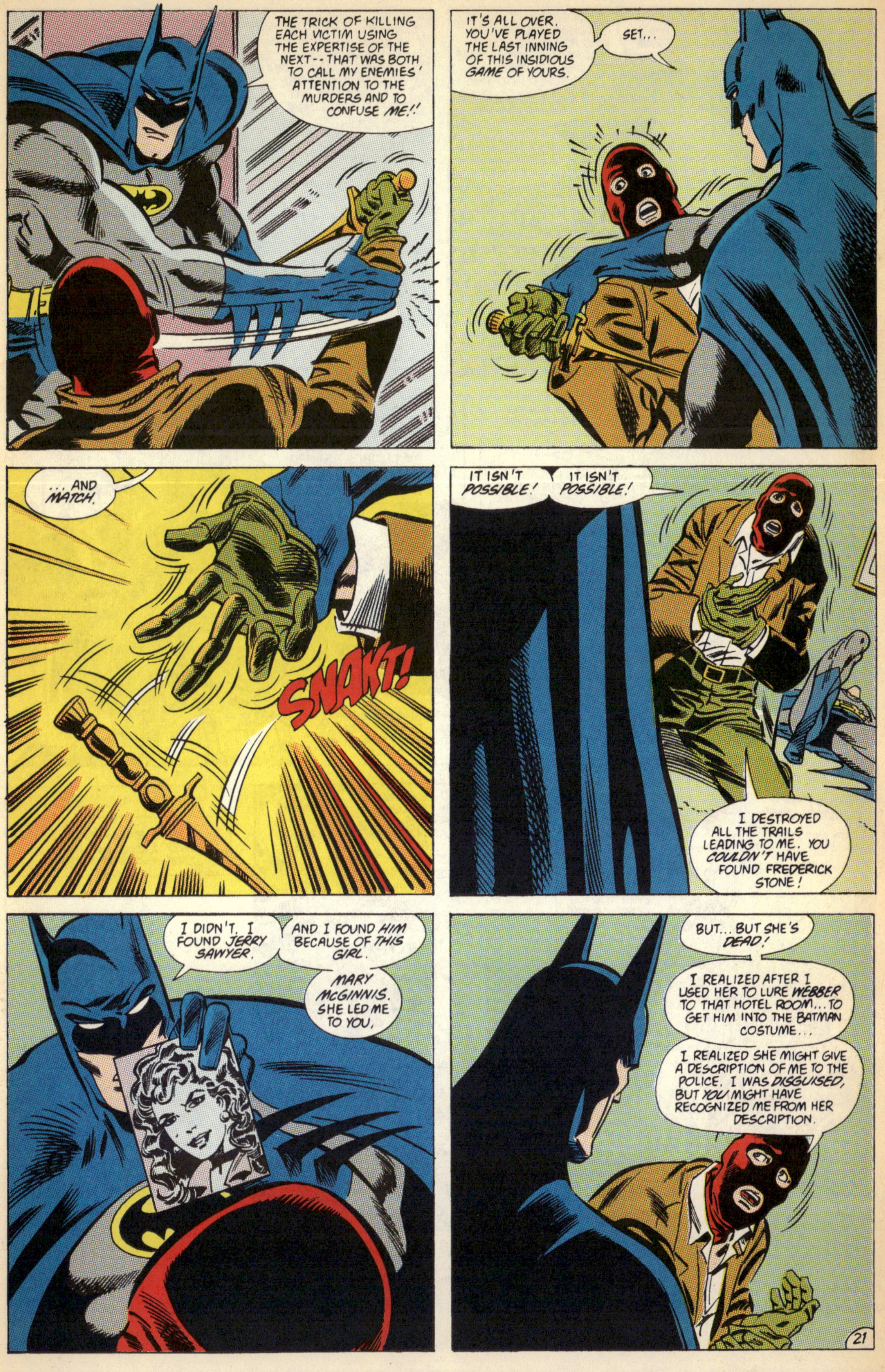
THE TRICK OF KILLING EACH VICTIM USING THE EXPERTISE OF THE NEXT-- THAT WAS BOTH TO CALL MY ENEMIES' ATTENTION TO THE MURDERS AND TO CONFUSE *ME*!!
IT'S ALL OVER. YOU'VE PLAYED THE LAST INNING OF THIS INSIDIOUS *GAME* OF YOURS.
SET...
... AND *MATCH*.
SNAKT!
IT ISN'T *POSSIBLE*!
IT ISN'T *POSSIBLE*!
I DESTROYED ALL THE TRAILS LEADING TO ME. YOU *COULDN'T* HAVE FOUND FREDERICK STONE!
I DIDN'T. I FOUND *JERRY SAWYER*.
AND I FOUND *HIM* BECAUSE OF *THIS* GIRL.
*MARY McGINNIS*. SHE LED ME TO YOU.
BUT... BUT SHE'S *DEAD*!
I REALIZED AFTER I USED HER TO LURE *WEBBER* TO THAT HOTEL ROOM... TO GET HIM INTO THE *BATMAN* COSTUME...
I REALIZED SHE MIGHT GIVE A DESCRIPTION OF ME TO THE POLICE. I WAS *DISGUISED*, BUT *YOU* MIGHT HAVE RECOGNIZED ME FROM HER DESCRIPTION.

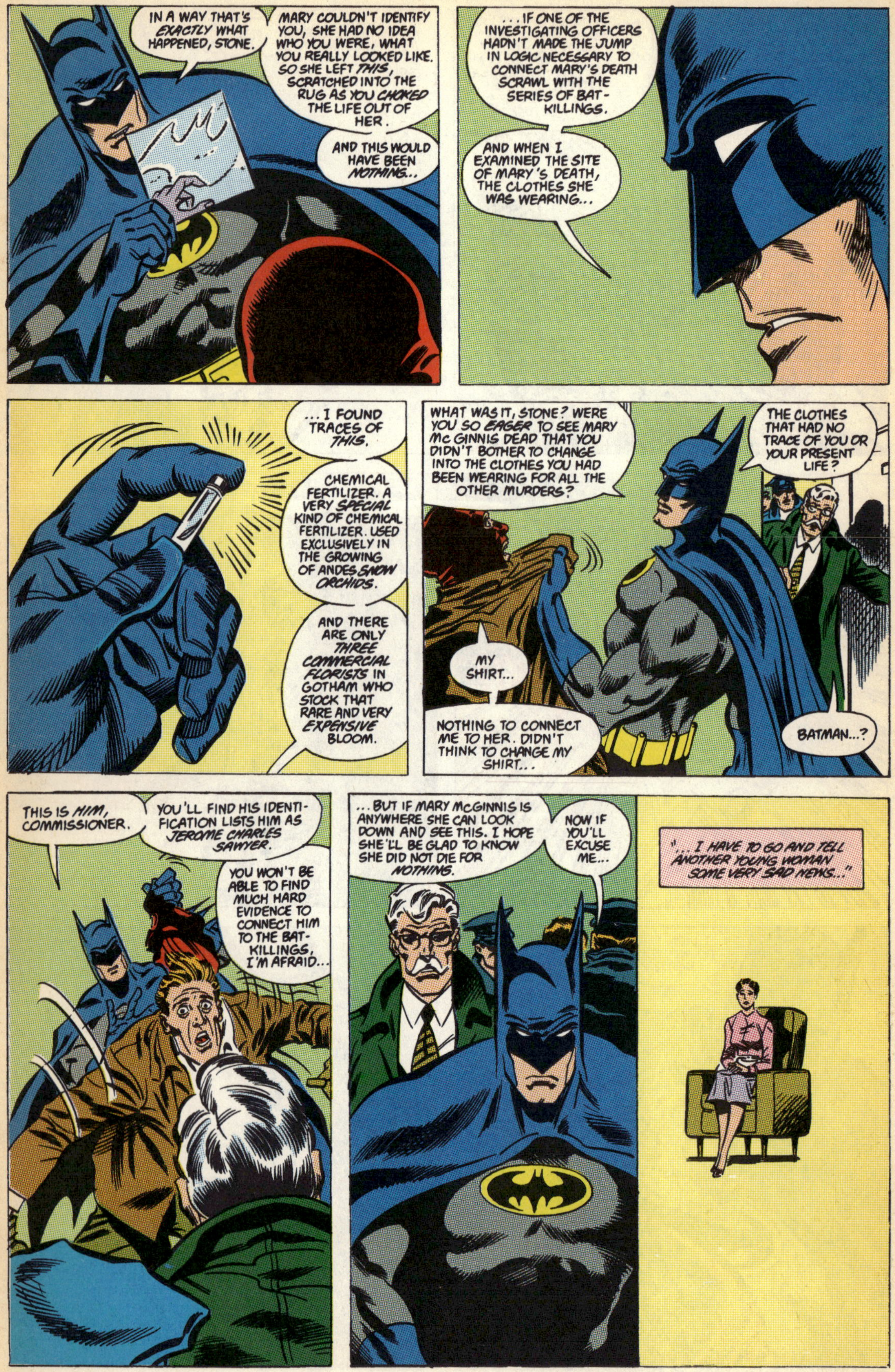
IN A WAY THAT'S EXACTLY WHAT HAPPENED, STONE.
MARY COULDN'T IDENTIFY YOU, SHE HAD NO IDEA WHO YOU WERE, WHAT YOU REALLY LOOKED LIKE. SO SHE LEFT THIS, SCRATCHED INTO THE RUG AS YOU CHOKED THE LIFE OUT OF HER.
AND THIS WOULD HAVE BEEN NOTHING...
...IF ONE OF THE INVESTIGATING OFFICERS HADN'T MADE THE JUMP IN LOGIC NECESSARY TO CONNECT MARY'S DEATH SCRAWL WITH THE SERIES OF BAT-KILLINGS.
AND WHEN I EXAMINED THE SITE OF MARY'S DEATH, THE CLOTHES SHE WAS WEARING...
...I FOUND TRACES OF THIS.
CHEMICAL FERTILIZER. A VERY SPECIAL KIND OF CHEMICAL FERTILIZER. USED EXCLUSIVELY IN THE GROWING OF ANDES SNOW ORCHIDS.
AND THERE ARE ONLY THREE COMMERCIAL FLORISTS IN GOTHAM WHO STOCK THAT RARE AND VERY EXPENSIVE BLOOM.
WHAT WAS IT, STONE? WERE YOU SO EAGER TO SEE MARY McGINNIS DEAD THAT YOU DIDN'T BOTHER TO CHANGE INTO THE CLOTHES YOU HAD BEEN WEARING FOR ALL THE OTHER MURDERS?
THE CLOTHES THAT HAD NO TRACE OF YOU OR YOUR PRESENT LIFE?
MY SHIRT...
NOTHING TO CONNECT ME TO HER. DIDN'T THINK TO CHANGE MY SHIRT...
BATMAN...?
THIS IS HIM, COMMISSIONER.
YOU'LL FIND HIS IDENTIFICATION LISTS HIM AS JEROME CHARLES SAWYER.
YOU WON'T BE ABLE TO FIND MUCH HARD EVIDENCE TO CONNECT HIM TO THE BAT-KILLINGS, I'M AFRAID...
...BUT IF MARY McGINNIS IS ANYWHERE SHE CAN LOOK DOWN AND SEE THIS, I HOPE SHE'LL BE GLAD TO KNOW SHE DID NOT DIE FOR NOTHING.
NOW IF YOU'LL EXCUSE ME...
"...I HAVE TO GO AND TELL ANOTHER YOUNG WOMAN SOME VERY SAD NEWS..."

# COVER GALLERY

DC
PART ONE OF THREE
THE MANY DEATHS OF THE
BATMAN
433
MAY 89
US 75¢
CAN 95¢
UK 50p
APPROVED BY THE COMICS CODE AUTHORITY
BYRNE • APARO • DECARLO

PART TWO OF THREE
THE MANY DEATHS OF THE
BATMAN
BYRNE • APARO • DeCARLO
434
JUN 89
US 75¢
CAN 95¢
UK 50p
APPROVED BY THE COMICS CODE AUTHORITY

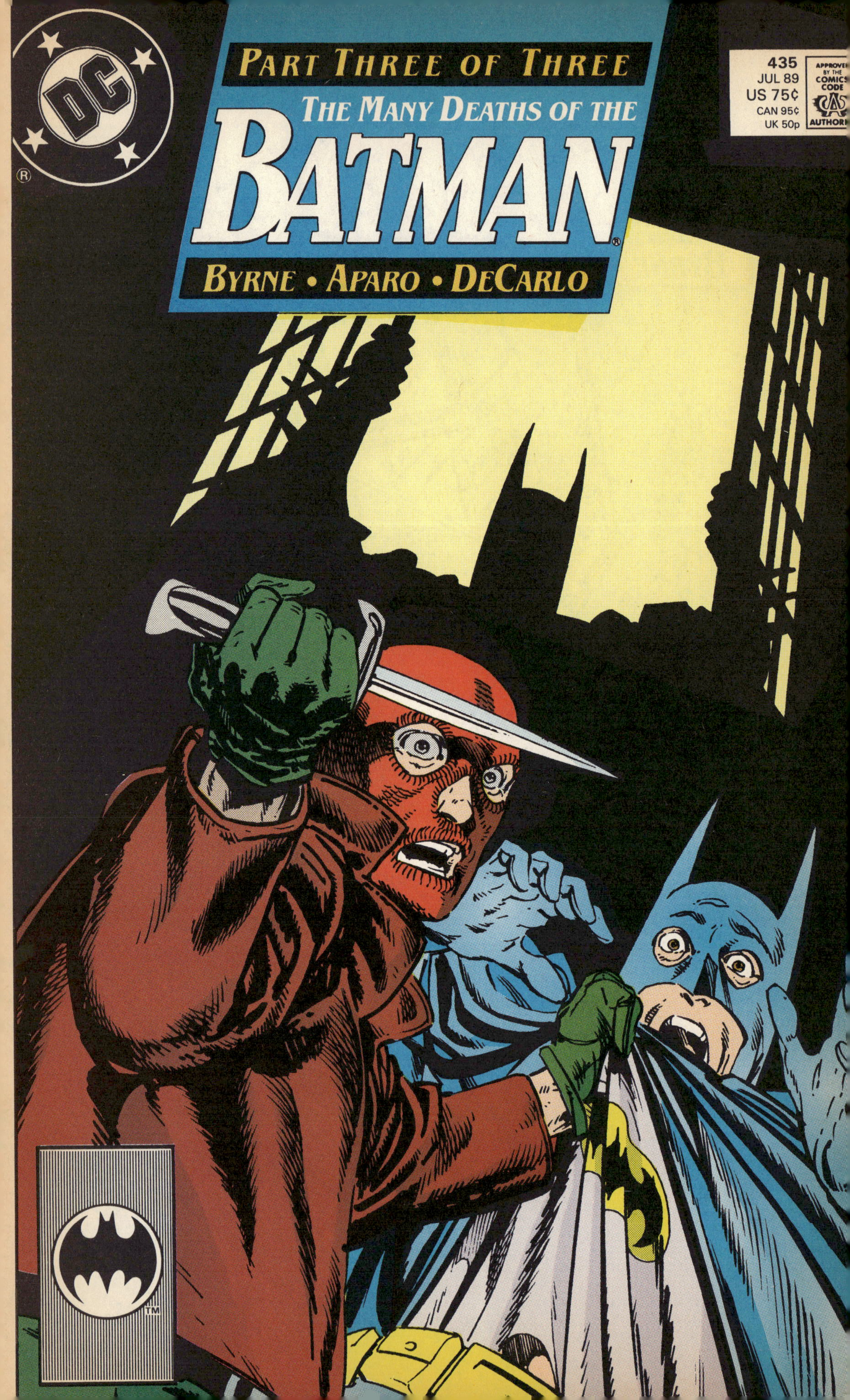
PART THREE OF THREE
THE MANY DEATHS OF THE
BATMAN
BYRNE • APARO • DECARLO
435
JUL 89
US 75¢
CAN 95¢
UK 50p

# BIOGRAPHIES

## JOHN BYRNE

John Byrne's first published work appeared in 1974 in the Charlton Comics series *Rog 2000*. Byrne left Charlton for Marvel Comics in 1975, making his debut there on *Iron Fist*. Over the last 16 years he has had a part in virtually every book in the line, with the exception of *Doctor Strange*. In 1985 he revamped the Superman legend with *The Man of Steel*. He is currently writing and pencilling *Namor* for Marvel, *Next Men* and *2112* for Dark Horse and *OMAC* for DC, as well as a yet untitled *Green Lantern* hardcover for DC.

## JIM APARO

Jim Aparo's first published comic book work also appeared in Charlton Comics with *Go-Go*, a kind of teenage rock and roll comic. From there he went on to do mystery, horror, and western stories. After several years he moved over to DC where he began pencilling *Aquaman* and *The Phantom Stranger* before he became the regular artist on *The Brave and the Bold*. After that series was cancelled he co-created *Batman and The Outsiders* with Mike Barr, which lasted until 1987. He was then asked to assume the pencilling chores of the regular *Batman* title until 1990 when the creative team was rotated over to *Detective Comics* where he is also inking and lettering his own pages.

## MIKE DECARLO

Mike DeCarlo entered the comics field in 1979 through enrollment in Dick Giordano's comic art course and began assisting him shortly thereafter and until 1981. His first credited inking job was *The Brave and the Bold*, April 1981. His other early credits include *Warlord, Green Lantern, Omega Men* and *Teen Titans*, followed by long runs on *Booster Gold, Legion of Super-Heroes, Batman* and *Detective Comics*. Currently he is working on *NFL SuperPro* for Marvel and will be inking a new ongoing series for DC scheduled for 1992 called *Salvo*.

# BATMAN BACKLIST

**BATMAN: TALES OF THE DEMON**
Dennis O'Neil/Dick Giordano/
Neal Adams/Bob Brown/
Dan Adkins/Don Newton/
Irv Novick/Michael Golden
ISBN: 0-930289-94-3
**$17.95 USA/$21.95 CAN**

**THE GREATEST BATMAN STORIES EVER TOLD**
ISBN: 0-930289-39-0
**$15.95 USA/$19.95 CAN**

**BATMAN: ARKHAM ASYLUM**
Grant Morrison/Dave McKean
ISBN: 0-930289-56-0
**$14.95 USA/$19.95 CAN**

**BATMAN: THE CULT**
Jim Starlin/Bernie Wrightson
ISBN: 0-930289-85-4
**$14.95 USA/$17.95 CAN**

**THE GREATEST JOKER STORIES EVER TOLD**
ISBN: 0-930289-36-6
**$14.95 USA/$19.95 CAN**

**BATMAN: THE DARK KNIGHT RETURNS**
Frank Miller/Lynn Varley/
Klaus Janson
ISBN: 0-930289-13-7
**$12.95 USA/$17.50 CAN**

**BATMAN: YEAR ONE**
Frank Miller/David Mazzucchelli
ISBN: 0-930289-33-1
**$9.95 USA/$12.95 CAN**

**BATMAN: YEAR TWO**
Mike W. Barr/Alan Davis/
Todd McFarlane/Paul Neary/
Alfredo Alcala
ISBN: 0-930289-49-8
**$9.95 USA/$12.95 CAN**

**CATWOMAN: HER SISTER'S KEEPER**
Mindy Newell/J.J. Birch/
Michael Blair
ISBN: 0-930289-97-8
**$9.95 USA/$12.95 CAN**

**ROBIN: A HERO REBORN**
Chuck Dixon/Tom Lyle/Bob Smith
ISBN: 1-56389-029-1
**$4.95 USA/$5.95 CAN**

**BATMAN: A DEATH IN THE FAMILY**
Jim Starlin/Jim Aparo/Mike DeCarlo
ISBN: 0-930289-44-7
**$3.95 USA/$4.95 CAN**

**BATMAN: A LONELY PLACE OF DYING**
Marv Wolfman/George Pérez/
Jim Aparo/Tom Grummett/
Mike DeCarlo/Bob McLeod
ISBN: 0-930289-63-3
**$3.95 USA/$4.95 CAN**

**BATMAN ARCHIVES Volume 1**
Bob Kane/Bill Finger/Gardner Fox/
Jerry Robinson/George Roussos
ISBN: 0-930289-60-9
**$39.95 USA/$49.95 CAN**

**BATMAN ARCHIVES Volume 2**
Bob Kane/Bill Finger/Jerry Robinson
ISBN: 1-56389-000-3
**$39.95 USA/$49.95 CAN**

**BATMAN: FULL CIRCLE**
Mike W. Barr/Alan Davis/Mark Farmer
ISBN: 0-930289-98-6
**$5.95 USA/$6.95 CAN**

**BATMAN MOVIE ADAPTATION**
Dennis O'Neil/Jerry Ordway
ISBN: 0-930289-46-3
**$4.95 USA/$6.50 CAN**

**BATMAN: GOTHAM BY GASLIGHT**
Brian Augustyn/Michael Mignola/
P. Craig Russell
ISBN: 0-930289-67-6
**$3.95 USA/$4.95 CAN**

**BATMAN: THE KILLING JOKE**
Alan Moore/Brian Bolland/
John Higgins
ISBN: 0-930289-45-5
**$3.95 USA/$4.95 CAN**

**BATMAN: DIGITAL JUSTICE**
Pepe Moreno
ISBN: 0-930289-87-0
**$24.95 USA/$30.95 CAN**

**BATMAN: BRIDE OF THE DEMON**
Mike W. Barr/Tom Grindberg/
Eva Grindberg
ISBN: 0-930289-79-X
**$19.95 USA/$23.95 CAN**

**BATMAN: SON OF THE DEMON**
Mike W. Barr/Jerry Bingham
ISBN: 0-930289-25-0
**$9.95 USA/$13.95 CAN**

**BATMAN 3-D**
John Byrne
ISBN: 0-930289-77-3
**$9.95 USA/$11.95 CAN**

**BATMAN/DRACULA: RED RAIN**
Doug Moench/Kelley Jones/
Malcolm Jones III
ISBN: 1-56389-012-7
**$24.95 USA/$29.95 CAN**

**BATMAN/JUDGE DREDD: JUDGMENT ON GOTHAM**
John Wagner/Alan Grant/
Simon Bisley
ISBN: 1-56389-022-4
**$5.95 USA/$6.95 CAN**

**BATMAN: BLIND JUSTICE**
Sam Hamm/Denys Cowan/
Dick Giordano
ISBN: 1-56389-047-X
**$7.50 USA/$9.00 CAN**

**BATMAN: MASTER OF THE FUTURE**
Brian Augustyn/Eduardo Barreto
ISBN: 1-56389-015-1
**$5.95 USA/$6.95 CAN**

**BATMAN: THE DAILIES Hardcover-Limited Edition**
ISBN: 0-87816-149-X
**$60.00 USA/$72.00 CAN**

**BATMAN: THE SUNDAY CLASSICS Hardcover-Limited Edition**
ISBN: 0-87816-163-5
**$75.00 USA/$96.00 CAN**

**BATMAN: HOLY TERROR**
Alan Brennert/Norm Breyfogle
ISBN: 1-56389-018-6
**$4.95 USA/$5.95 CAN**